WILLIAM BOGGS

SIN BOLDLY

But trust God more boldly still

ABINGDON PRESS

Nashville

SIN BOLDLY

This book is printed on acid-free paper.

Library of Congress Cataloging-in-Publication Data

Boggs, William, 1947–
    Sin boldly: but trust God more boldly still / William Boggs.
        p. cm.
    ISBN 0-687-38535-0 (alk. paper)
        1. Grace (Theology) 2. Christian life—Methodist authors.
    I. Title.
    BT761.2.B64   1990
    234-dc20
                                                        89-35390
                                                        CIP

Scripture quotations noted NIV are taken from the *Holy Bible: New
International Version*. Copyright © 1973, 1978, 1984 by the
International Bible Society. Used by permission of Zondervan Bible
Publishers.

Scripture quotations noted RSV are from the Revised Standard
Version of the Bible, copyright 1946, 1952, 1971 by the Division of
Christian Education of the National Council of Churches of Christ in
the U.S.A. Used by permission.

The scripture quotation noted *TLB* is from *The Living Bible*, copyright
© 1971 by Tyndale House Publishers, Wheaton, Ill. Used by
permission.

Other quotations are paraphrases or are taken from the Authorized
Version of the Bible.

MANUFACTURED IN THE UNITED STATES OF AMERICA

Acknowledgments

Thanks are due so many people, I scarcely know where to start. My mother, Mrs. Gerline Boggs, taught me the first lessons about Christ and the church, and years of theological studies haven't improved much on her basic wisdom. My brother, Bobby Wayne, my sisters, Mary Jean and Brenda Faye, have all been helpful in reading the manuscript and refreshing my memory where needed. They will be completely appalled that I have referred to them by both their first and middle names, but that's what they were called as children, and we are still children to one another.

Mark and Susan Malter have been close friends for a long time. Both of them read the manuscript and gave encouragement from the very beginning.

The Reverend Virginia Wheeler and the Reverend Patricia Farris both gave their valuable theological insights and helped me keep the language as nonsexist as possible.

Professors like Ray Dunning, Neil Wiseman, Bill Muehl, and Leon Watts were influential in my formation as a minister. I hope they are not completely appalled at how my theology has turned out.

Finally, I wish to express my gratitude to Roland and Jerre Brammeier. They believed in me when others didn't and supported my ministry. Roland represents the United Methodist District Superintendency at its finest.

To my children, Tanya, Benjamin, and Justin,
with all my love

CONTENTS

Introduction

What a strange thing it is to be writing these words to you realizing that I will never get to know you, but you will come to know things about me that I would never dare tell you in a face-to-face conversation. I am, like most preachers, not the most honest person in the world. I conceal myself behind a flurry of funny stories and a barrage of ancient wisdom. I present a facade of wholeness while teaching and counseling others about living with integrity.

I hope to God that something with a passing resemblance to truth manages to sandwich itself between the covers of this book. But, because I must drag along my own humanity, like a two-hundred-pound ball and chain, writing this has been, like swimming, a matter of trying to keep my own head above water while hoping to save someone else whose frantic struggle for life may be more than enough to drown us both.

I decided a long time ago that, while preaching is *formally* about telling the truth, it is *essentially* a story about the struggle of the preacher and the people to discover life itself. Along the way something about God may or may not be revealed. Preaching probably obscures as much of God as it reveals, in the same way that every person who calls himself or herself a Christian is both a living example of God's grace and a walking bundle of contradictions to the presence of Christ in the world.

For better or worse, I'm a preacher, and most days I wouldn't want to be anything else. Monday is the exception. Every week, without fail, I suffer from the postpartum blues. The baby has been delivered. I'm not certain it looks anything like me, and I get horribly depressed. Every Monday I quit, and promise myself I'll try to find a decent job. But, by Tuesday morning it's time for the men's prayer breakfast, and they serve a great bowl of oatmeal with raisins. Anyway, preaching is the only job in town where you labor for just an hour a week—inside work, no heavy lifting.

Like all the rest of the preachers, I figured that if I could write sermons week after week, surely to goodness I could write a book. Little did I know when I set out to write a book about grace that I would encounter so many of my own well-entrenched sins to accuse me.

Most of this material came from the life I shared with the congregation of the Wilshire United Methodist Church in Los Angeles, California. It isn't particularly timeless theology; I gave up on that after trying, unsuccessfully, to convince my seminary professors that I actually understood Paul Tillich. I hope that in one way or another this book is simply about life. My life, your life, the life of my family, the life of the people I pastor (and who, as often as not, pastor me). If the truth, with a capital T, is told in the process, I am grateful, but not wholly responsible.

Frederick Buechner has influenced my ministry more than I can say. He delivered the Lyman Beecher Lectures on preaching while I was a student at the Yale Divinity School. Those lectures overwhelmed me. At times I forgot to breathe and I would find myself leaning forward, holding in my breath, and listening with my whole body. "Telling the Truth: The Gospel as Tragedy, Comedy and Fairytale" was his topic, but the subject was life—his life, my life, your life, the life that exploded out of eternity and changed the meaning of life forever. Since then I have read his books, most of them several times, and attempted, in my own way, to preach as honestly as I knew how. I have not always succeeded. In fact, there have been times when my cowardice turned the sermon to dust in my mouth, and I sneaked out of the fellowship hall after church, to go home and sleep another one off.

Of all the topics I might have chosen, grace is the most seductive. The temptation is to sugarcoat the gospel so that it goes down easier. Grace is certainly the tastiest doctrine on the church's menu. I am hoping that I haven't made grace sound so unrealistic it becomes just preacher-talk, or so diluted that it sounds like warmed over psychology. I struggle to put the pieces of my own life together in an honest way. Sometimes, on good days, the pieces seem to form a whole, and sometimes on very good days, the pieces even seem to make sense.

I am writing this while hidden away at the Quail Mountain Ranch in Santa Maria, California. Q.M.R. has become a special place for me and my children. Through the kindness of my good friends David and Kimberly Farrar we come here to escape from the pressures of Los Angeles and the demands of pastoring a large, urban church.

On this trip I am alone. When you're alone at Q.M.R., you're really alone, surrounded by miles and miles of rolling hills, a sky full of evening stars, and, occasionally, the mournful cry of a coyote, who sounds as if he needs a pastoral call. Earlier, I unpacked the car of books, old sermon folders, unfinished chapters of *the* book, and my personal computer, then set out to finally confront the task of finishing this work. In a deeper sense I am the one who must be confronted: me, the social one who seizes on people as an escape from the frightening task of facing my own demons, the frantic one who flees into busyness as a refuge from solitude, the deceptive one who uses sleight-of-hand relationships as a tool for my own selfishness. After only a few hours at the ranch, I was frightened by the stillness, slightly depressed, and restless.

A crusty old woman from the ranch up the road dropped in unexpectedly. I was fixing my favorite ranch supper when she tapped on the front door and invited herself in, saying, "You're from Los Angeles, aren't you?" She looked around the living room, chuckled, and inspected me closely, taking in my shirtless chest, my baggy khaki shorts, and my tousled hair.

"Whatcha doin' here?" she demanded, peering out from under her straw hat like a hawk about to swoop down on her prey.

"Right now, I'm cooking chili," was my inane reply.

"Great—I love chili," she chuckled as she wandered my way, into the kitchen.

"I'm senile you know," she confided, and I was tempted to shoot back, "No kidding," but held my tongue.

I offered her a spoonful of my pride and joy, but no sooner had she taken a taste than she turned to the trash can and spat it out, cackling, "You do like hot stuff, don't you?"

Turning to find her way back out the front door, she glanced around the house and, spotting my computer, asked, "What's that?"

As I explained about word processing and my plan to spend a few days writing, she interrupted to ask, "Are you gonna put me in the book?" I shifted uncomfortably, suddenly aware of the feel of the cool oak boards beneath my bare feet.

"What's the book about?" she snapped.

"Grace," I replied laconically, praying fervently she would leave soon.

"What's that?"

"God's grace," I mumbled, angry that I had come here to be alone and she was asking me questions I wasn't sure I could answer. "You know, the sense in which God loves each one of us."

The woman stood silhouetted against the waning light in the front door, as tough as leather and as wrinkled as a dried peach. She looked around again, taking in the turn-of-the-century ranch house with its eclectic, weekends-only decorations, and, looking back at me for a moment, snorted, "So what?"

Without further adieu, she walked down the gravel drive, climbed into a brand new Mercedes Benz, and rolling down her electric window as she pulled away, said, "Stop by if it gets too quiet. We're just a few miles up the road. We're only country folk, but you're welcome."

California people still seem a little strange to me, at times.

Long after she incongruously drove away, her question haunted me: "So what?" So what if God loves us? How does that help us pay the bills, raise the kids, or make it through another day of monotonous desperation? I began seriously to doubt that the woman was senile, and after a while I began to doubt that she had been real. Perhaps the silence was already getting to me. My mind could not seem to shut the question out. So what? So what? So what? So what!

It seems to me that grace *is* the "so what" of God's love. To say that God loves us is fine as far as it goes. But grace is the very practical, life-oriented dimension of love. It has been classically defined as "God's wholly unmerited favor." Put another way, grace means God is for us. Tillich went so far as to declare that our only response is to "accept our acceptance," and that's hard to improve on.

God's grace is a radical acceptance that does not blink at our many shortcomings, failures, and sins, but extends divine favor to forgive us, empower us, and to sustain us. Inevitably, if we can accept this acceptance, we are changed. Not all at once, to be sure, and certainly not easily. Nevertheless, we are changed when we see that God loves us, has loved us all along, and, as we are promised, will go right on loving us.

God loves us—so we are accepted. God is for us—so we are empowered. God gave Jesus to us—so we are forgiven. God is with us—so we are sustained. All these are ways of saying the same thing. We are graced, to make it a verb, which it has been all along, anyway.

Chapter One

In the Beginning

There is a distant place I once knew, filled with the sweet smell of Carolina pines, the breathtaking blue expanse of unpolluted sky, the clammy touch of humidity that tries to compete with temperature, and the piercing chill of a secret stream that I once fancied no one had ever swum naked before Johnny Cooper and I dropped our cut-off jeans in the bushes and spent a mischievous afternoon flaunting our inno-cence in a skinny-dipped swimming hole that we call to this day, simply, Cold Creek.

In unexpected moments my memory takes me once again to my own secret garden of grace. A place of sandy Carolina roads, acres thick with pine trees, and the unforgettable sounds of the Supremes, the Temptations, and Elvis Presley, playing on the radio of my daddy's red pickup truck with an Easy Rider Rifle Rack in the rear window. It was a time before time began for me; a time before television introduced me to Roy Rogers, Pinky Lee, and a world beyond my world that I had never dreamed existed. It was a time before Vietnam, a time before it was necessary to compete and achieve, a time before I discovered that my family was poor, a time before death was real, a time before betrayal and disappointment, a time before sin existed.

I had heard about sin, of course. Our preachers thundered on and on about the horrors of sin. But mostly sin was dancing with girls, which held no appeal for me, and movies, which were beyond my financial resources and only existed in Augusta anyway, twenty miles distant, but it might as well have been two thousand. The only sinners I knew were my Uncle Homer, who drank beer at an outrageous redneck bar called the Dew Drop Inn, and my father, who smoked Camel cigarettes. I vaguely remember the preachers glaring out across the pulpit at us, pointing toward the back of the small church where the kids sat, and saying with sad certainty, "The wages of sin are death." I didn't have the faintest idea what that meant, but time certainly proved the preachers to be right since Uncle Homer died of cirrhosis of the liver and Dad died of lung cancer.

It was a time before time, a time before the world existed beyond that small-town Eden of mine, a time before sin meant anything more than loud preacher-talk, a time before death claimed anyone that I loved—which brings me to my Grandpa Boggs.

As I think about my own story of grace, for me the closest thing to God was John Walter Boggs. He lived with us then. A hard, crusty old man, who was curt with my father and my uncle, polite to my mother, and absolutely, eternally loving toward me. He had not always been blind, just as he had not always been old, but I had only known him as such, so for me he always was and always will be a blind old man.

A blind God isn't much of a contradiction for me. When you look around at the world as you and I know it, if God isn't blind then surely there must be many days when blindness would be preferable to seeing the infinite varieties of madness and chaos that humanity has created.

I am old enough now to know that Grandpa Boggs loved me so intensely and showed me such unreserved affection because he had never been able to show that kind of love to my father. Loving my father's son was a way of making up for the anguish of their relationship. Age brings certain privileges, and one of those most cherished by old men is the chance to put aside their reserve and their busyness to love a small child.

He died . . . and I remember his death clearly, because of the miracle that occurred just before he died, the one and only genuine, certifiable miracle I have witnessed. After nearly twenty years of blindness, Grandpa Boggs was pretty much resigned to his condition. In fact, he would tell you quickly that the way the world was going he didn't much care to see it anyway, and most folks weren't worth looking at (but anytime he said that, he would softly stroke my hair as if to reassure me that present company was excepted). There was one regret for him. He had never seen his grandson. That didn't matter much to me because he had loved me enough to make up for it, but it mattered to him a great deal.

Now, before telling you about the miracle, I should tell you Grandpa Boggs was not a religious man in the traditional sense of the word. But in so many ways he was deeply religious. He didn't care for churches and organized religion except for church picnics, which we called dinner-on-the-ground. He listened for hour after hour as my mother read the Bible aloud to him, but he never cared much for preachers. He believed preachers always messed up the Bible when they tried to preach about it, and added to it here and there to suit their own private prejudices, a failing unfortunately still with us. He loved the Bible—loved its stories, loved its drama, loved its realism. He marveled at its miracle stories, and would sometimes turn to me and say, "Boy do you believe that story?" I would solemnly nod, and he would absently mutter, "Of course you do. So do I."

What he wanted more than anything in the world was to see me before he died. He didn't pray a lot, but he prayed for that. He must have sensed death closing in on him, because he began to pray more intensely for the Lord to give him sight, just long enough to see his grandson before he died.

That was of course an impossibility because his eyes had long since turned a milky blue from the disease that brought his long journey into night. He was willing to try anything that might give him a few minutes of sight, so several times we took him to faith healing services in huge canvas tents that came to our small town. It just didn't work because he would start fuming about the way people make "damn fools" of themselves during these religious carnivals, and of course, even Oral Roberts couldn't do much with somebody like that.

Then one day, in our backyard, while he and I were playing together, he could see. I am almost embarrassed to tell the story because it seems so improbable, but for just a few minutes he could see. He hollered to my mother to come quickly, and in his ecstasy even called to his sons, a miracle in itself. Everybody came tearing into the yard to see what the fuss was all about and quickly grew quiet as it became apparent that he could see.

It was long ago, before time began for me. I still remember my intense joy, my sense of excitement and awe. He kissed my mother, then, miracle of all miracles, embraced my father, hugged my Uncle Homer, who was too drunk to be certain that it was real, and then picked me up and stared at me with an intensity that frightened me. I remember holding his face between my small hands while both of us cried, and then in the most frightening moment of all he saw something in me. The story is already unbelievable, so I suppose it won't be any more incredible when I tell you that he looked me in the eyes and softly said, "A preacher." That was all. Just those two words so quietly uttered with a tone of surprise and thirty years later I wonder which was the greater miracle—that he could see or that he could see something so deeply hidden in me and in my distant future. But he saw me for just a few minutes. He saw something so incredible that even though the words stuck in his throat he said them anyway . . . "A preacher."

The psychologist in me has spent a good many years

explaining away the miracle, in the same way that the psychologist in me argues that if he had said "A lawyer" in the same tone of amazement and love I would probably be persuading juries today instead of telling stories to people who judge them with the same hope for the truth and nothing but the truth that any good jury looks for. My Sigmund Freud alter ego is certain that the child was so impressionable and the old man's love so intense that it was a foregone conclusion that the old man could delude himself into believing that he really could see for just those few minutes and the child could never hope to do anything else but fulfill the prophecy so lovingly uttered.

A boy being held in an old man's arms, holding the ancient face between his chubby, grimy hands, in a time before time began for me, on an afternoon when my only miracle happened. And now you have the story. The interval of years between the boy that I was and the man that I have become has been marked by long stretches of blind wandering and only occasional places of clarity. From that small Southern town to the Marine Corps at seventeen, then into the dry world of corporate success, and finally, desperately into the ministry. But always for me, the beginning must be told as the story of an old man who loved me blindly, and saw me with a vision that had nothing to do with optical nerves. It remains a moment of grace for me, a haunting presence in my memory. I tell you this to say that grace has about it a feeling of inexplicable mystery. It is essentially a moment or a series of moments in which our blinded eyes can see and a new vision of life opens before us.

The door to our lost garden of grace may not be blocked by an angel with a flaming sword as the biblical story has it, but it is blocked nevertheless. Thomas Wolfe was right; we can never go home again. The way is hindered by too many degrees from ivy-covered schools, my too tidy world of Los Angeles sophistication, and above all my certain knowledge of my own dark sinfulness. Time has begun for us all, and who knows how short it may be.

This thing we call life flows on for all of us, and into this time that we have been given there come moments when God's presence becomes piercingly known to us. The light of these grace-filled moments enables us to view ourselves in a different perspective and we realize with the shock of sudden awareness that God has been active in our lives all along, quietly, steadily giving us strength and power.

Because theologians have a great investment in finding just the right words to describe the human experience of God, we made up a phrase for this. It's called prevenient grace. *Prevenient* is not a commonly used word. In fact, I had never heard of it until I studied it in seminary, and I have seldom heard it used since then. That's a shame because it's such a wonderful word, once you understand it.

You will notice immediately the similarity between prevenient and another word: *preventive*. Prevenient grace is a preventive form of grace that comes to us between conception and conversion to prevent us from moving so far from God, in our sin, that we could not respond to the wooing of the Holy Spirit working to bring us into a relationship with God. If grace means God is for us, then prevenient means God has always been for us—right from the beginning.

At every step of our life, God has been for us. Even if we don't know it or acknowledge it, even if we don't act like it, even if we have made no claims to loving God, God has been for us all along.

Paul's letter to the church at Ephesus contains a passage that describes this process. "As for you, you were dead in your . . . sins. . . . But because of his great love for us, God, who is rich in mercy, made us alive with Christ even when we were dead in transgressions—it is by grace you have been saved" (2:1, 4-5 NIV).

No one has to convince us of our sinfulness. In the deepest part of our lives, we know it. In the quiet stillness of our inner selves, each one of us knows what it is to sin, to fail the ones we love the most, to fail ourselves, to fail God, to be less than we ought to be, to be less than we could be, to be cowards in the face of immorality, to be silent in the presence of injustice. Lately I have found the courage to admit that there are some things I believe in passionately, but I don't always live up to them. That is difficult to say about myself, but it's true. It seems to be true for the people I counsel. I assume it is true for everybody, maybe even for you.

We know about being estranged from one another. We know about being estranged from God. Paul says, "All have sinned and come short of the glory of God." But he goes on to say a wonderful thing. God doesn't give up on us—not ever! For whatever direction our lives may take, prevenient grace is our assurance that God's love prevents us from going so far that we cannot respond to God. Love, mercy, and grace are always extended to us.

God has, of course, been loving us all along and pursuing us throughout our lives. We are unaware of this, because, God knows, we are blind, and seem to prefer blindness to life in the light of God's grace. But, unpredictably, and unexpectedly, we have moments of quiet awareness, times when we are able to see a power at work in our lives. These may be moments of panicky crisis when anxiety holds us in its unrelenting grip. Sometimes they are moments of sheer joy and unexpected happiness. Once in a while, even in the simple stillness of a quiet moment when we are alone inside our skin and the world seems hushed with mystery, surrounding us like a soft, gentle rain, we sense a presence beyond ourselves; and if we were only quick enough to glance out of the corner of our clouded eyes we might see the disappearing back of One who is Grace, the God who has slipped into the back door of our existence because we did not answer the faint knock at the front door. These are moments of grace, when the fragments of seemingly unrelated events come together and, sometimes, occasionally, once in a great while, for a moment, meaning and direction are available for us.

Grace opens our eyes to our lives in a startling way. Look at your life. "All moments are key moments," says Frederick Buechner. All moments are moments of grace. In every moment God is trying to show you something, to lead you somewhere, to make you into a new person. In every event, there is a redemptive, creative possibility, if we only have eyes to see it.

It's an old Wesleyan word, prevenient, and it's a good word. We will examine several descriptive words that can be used for grace, words like *prevenient, justifying, sanctifying, sustaining,* and *sacramental.* These words do not refer to different *kinds* of grace, only to different moments in time, and to the different forms and functions that grace has in our lives. Above all, these words attached to grace describe it as a process that permeates our lives through and through.

Prevenient grace comes to us through parents, relatives, friends, and events. Sometimes grace is given to us even through our sin. My blind grandfather, my praying mother, my unpredictable children, my good friends, the communities of faith to which I have belonged, and my moments of terrible failure and ecstatic joy have all been channels through which God's grace has come to me. Before our awareness or acceptance of a relationship with God, grace is active, it goes before us.

Which brings me to my youngest son, Justin. When he was three years old, he decided he didn't love me. He is a tough little cookie who is rather standoffish around strangers. He "hates" people who pat him on the head and ask him to smile. In fact, he's been known to kick them for their trouble, which is not the best P.R. for a pastor. Justin wears mischief like a well-tailored suit.

Freud called this the Oedipal phase. Justin wanted

more and more of his mother's attention and seemed to feel that he competed with me to get it. I rather enjoyed seeing it—most of the time, because I treasure Justin's strength and determination—most of the time.

Justin would swagger up to me and with a gleam of challenge in his eye, say, "I don't love you. I love Mommy." I consoled myself by realizing that you have to love somebody quite a lot to keep saying, "I don't love you." It just takes a lot of energy.

Every night when I get home, no matter how late it is, I go in and kiss my children good night. It's just about my favorite thing to do. Sometimes I sit and talk softly to them, even though they are asleep. Tanya, Benjamin, and Justin know that every night I'll either tuck them in before they go to sleep, or sit with them for a moment if they are already asleep.

One night, during Justin's guerrilla warfare, I went into the boys' room after they were asleep, and sat down on Justin's bed. As I leaned over to kiss him good night, sensing that it was me, he rolled away and muttered, "I don't love you." I just touched his tousled hair, and whispered, "But I love you, Justin."

As I got ready for bed, my wife, Reva, and I laughed about the incident. Then, around 4:00 A.M., Justin apparently had a nightmare. He began to cry out. Soon, he got out of his bed and I could hear the sound of three-year-old feet coming down the hall, then into our room.

I covertly watched him come cautiously into the room, checking the terrain for possible ambushes. He looked so small and vulnerable but came forward with the stealth of a seasoned warrior and stood at the foot of our bed, trying to decide whose side of the bed to crawl into. I should explain that Justin knew that if he crawled in by his mommy she would send him back to his own bed, unless he was very ill. But Daddy, for all his other faults, will usually accommodate a little person.

I watched him standing there, making his choice. He padded around to my side of the bed and, rubbing his eyes, climbed under the covers beside me in the darkness. As he crawled in and snuggled into my body, he reached up and moved my arm so that it would cradle his head. Then he rolled over, snuggled closer, and softly said, "I still don't love you."

I lay awake a long time, holding him in my arms, loving him so much it hurt, and thinking about a God who loves us so much it hurts. Even when we nailed love to a cross, God's grace overcame the force of evil and raised Jesus from the dead. Even when we say we don't love God, even when we push and struggle against the awful responsibility that love places on us, we are held in the loving arms of God and nothing can separate us from that.

Grace is prevenient. It comes to us first. It holds us in the arms of God throughout our lives. God loved us first with a power that cannot be denied. When our eyes are opened we can see this, if only for a fleeting instant, and a new vision for our lives becomes possible. So Tillich could say, "Here and there in the world and now and then in ourselves is a New Creation, usually hidden, but sometimes manifest and certainly manifest in Jesus who is called the Christ."

Chapter Two

Without One Plea

Growing up poor is one of the most romanticized experiences in American mythology. The country that produced Horatio Alger has built a library of stories in which the poor, ragged young hero finds golden opportunities and becomes enormously successful.

The strange thing about being raised in "poverty" is that you don't know you're poor. There was always enough food in our house, although often it was only beans and cornbread, until Sunday dinner came along with fried chicken and mashed potatoes. There was heat in the winter, Cold Creek in the summer, and the Carolina woods were full of indians and pirates.

That was shattered one day when I was about twelve years old. I remember the school bus pulling up in front of my house, and me gathering my books to get off. As I got up from my seat and walked to the front of the bus, I passed the prettiest girl in the sixth grade. (Remember her?) By then I had learned to notice those things, although, naturally, after ordination I conquered the habit. She glanced from our small house to my plain but clean clothes and I overheard her whisper, "Those people are pore." (Only rich people say "poor.")

I went inside our house, nearly in tears, and asked, "Mom, are we pore?"

My mother paused a moment, standing at the kitchen stove, and said, "Not in the things that really count." But I knew with a red-faced certainty that everyone didn't agree.

That was my first encounter with shame. All of us, of course, have felt shame, but it seemed to dominate *my* teenage years. I went to work shortly after discovering we were poor. In my first job, I dipped snowballs in the back of a truck driven by our underpaid preacher. He drove slowly through our small town ringing an old cow bell that called sweaty children from their summer games to a moment of ice cold delight. I never joined their chases again. Instead I poured grape and cherry syrup over neatly rounded scoops of shaved ice in paper cones. I wanted to earn my own way.

I used all my money to buy clothes. I studied the way other children dressed, because the only things I knew were jeans and flannel shirts. Imagine my surprise on moving to Los Angeles twenty years later and discovering that jeans and flannel shirts were the marks of affluence, often worn by people driving Jaguars and Rolls Royces. The world does turn round doesn't it.

My father became the most conspicuous source of my shame. He was a blunt, coarse construction worker who wore overalls and faded blue workshirts.

His nails were dirty and his shoes were steel-toed work boots that we called brogans. As far as I know, Dad wore a tie on the day he was married and on the day we buried him. He never trusted people who didn't work with their hands. Papa once said wearing a tie cut off the circulation of blood to the head and if I didn't believe it I should listen to the braying of all those brain-damaged jackasses who wore ties around their necks.

I dreaded going to town with him because I had spent all my money on nice clothes and studied other people in order to learn good manners, but he delighted in wearing dirty carpenter's overalls and saying the most outrageous things.

One day we were in the grocery store together. It was called Piggly Wiggly, but he always referred to it as Hoggly Woggly, and to this day when I'm home that's what I call it. While browsing through the magazines, I encountered one of my new friends. I was confident that my khaki trousers, Gant madras shirt, and Bass Weejun pennyloafers were correct, but I silently prayed that my friend would leave before Dad made it to the cash register.

To my horror, I couldn't get my friend out of the store in time. As Dad prepared to pay for his few groceries, the cashier apparently overcharged him, and an argument ensued. Dad loved a good fight. He ended the dispute, turning every head in the store when he loudly said, "Lady, you ain't got the brains God promised a billy goat."

My friend giggled and whispered, "Who is that clod?"

With my face on fire, I said, "I don't know. Let's get out of here before he starts trouble." I walked home alone, dreading to face Dad and explain why I didn't wait for him.

More than twenty years later as I stood at his grave, I remembered my shame, compounded now by guilt and regret. Too late in my life, I realized how much my father had given me. He taught me that position in life is no guarantee of character and that truth does not depend on fancy words for its efficacy. He knew that who you are is more important than what you do for a living. As we lowered him into the bright-red Carolina clay, I said with gratitude what my mother had said to me so many years before: "He was not poor in the things that matter most."

Shame and guilt are common human experiences. We spend a lot of time, energy, and money trying to keep up appearances. Deep inside, so many of us are uncertain and insecure. Too many of us live our lives for nothing more significant than to become the Vice-president of Anything. We believe that bigger offices always contain bigger people. But the sad truth is that most of us never quite make it. I've discovered that most people who seem to be making it are just bumping around in their big offices and homes, still frightened and feeling more than a little phony. We are the hidden people, or, even more frightening, perhaps T. S. Eliot was right when he called us the "straw men." We are scared, working like hell to make ourselves feel better, but never quite succeeding.

How do we deal with the hollow darkness of our lives? How do we live constructively with those hidden places within us that accuse us and remain sources of fear and anxiety? Jung accurately observed that the brighter our persona (the face we show to the world), the darker our shadow (the hidden self). What does the Christian faith offer that helps us hold life together creatively and with integrity? Something called justifying grace.

Making justifying grace operative in human life is quite a challenge for the church. It is undoubtedly one of the most pivotal ideas in the history of theology, standing as it does at the very center of Jewish, Protestant, and Catholic dialogue. The word *justify* is a legal term that means "to pronounce free from guilt; to absolve." Did you get that? There is a way to be pronounced free from our guilt; God has made provisions to absolve us.

Because this problem has been a part of the human dilemma from the very beginning of time, it isn't surprising that one of the oldest biblical stories illuminates the issue.

This is the Boggs version: God was walking in the cool of the evening, and looking around, noticed that Adam and Eve were conspicuous by their absence. So God called out, "Where in the world are you?"

Adam, standing tactfully behind an azalea bush, nervously answered, "We were naked so we hid ourselves." Enter shame.

"Oh yeah," said God, who had made them in the first place and wasn't the least bit embarrassed by how they looked with their clothes off, "who told you about naked?"

Notice how quickly Adam learns the meaning of

blame. "The *woman*, whom *you* gave me, made me eat the fruit from the Tree of Knowledge."

God has never liked excuses and to this day wonders who invented them, so God said, "Did she hold a gun to your head, Adam?"

Getting more uneasy by the minute, Adam giggled, "What's a gun, Lord? That's a good word, we can use it later, but right now we're only up to fructose."

Anticipating the next question, and comedian Flip Wilson by millions of years, Eve cried, "The devil made me do it."

Satan, dressed up like a serpent for the First Annual Eden Costume Ball, shrugged and said, "I haven't got a leg to stand on." (I know snakes can't shrug, but it strengthens a weak punch line. Consider it a metaphor.)

The act of disobedience was sinful because it alienated Adam from God. By refusing to accept responsibility for his own action, Adam became alienated from himself. By blaming Eve, Adam became alienated from her. Far from being a moralistic myth, the story powerfully illustrates alienation as the form sin takes. Shame, compounded by guilt, resulting in alienation from self, others, and God; "the wages of sin are death."

The epistle of I John contains a verse that goes to the heart of this matter and offers us an alternative to our self-destructive alienation. We are promised, "If we confess our sins, [God] is faithful and just to forgive us *our* sins, and to cleanse us from all unrighteousness." That is not only good sermon material, it is the stuff of which new creations are made.

Forgiveness is the bedrock upon which justifying grace is built. In our discussion of prevenient grace, we saw that God has always been for us, right from the beginning, and that God loved us, before any awareness on our part. Now we are able to see the very specific function of justifying grace. It is the means by which we encounter God's forgiveness as a remedy to our shame, our guilt, and the resulting alienation.

Confessing our sins in no way purchases God's forgiveness; it does however allow us to experience that forgiveness existentially. God has already forgiven us, because in Christ we have already been reconciled to God, but the forgiveness does not become real until we discover it to be true for ourselves. Protestants have disdained the use of confession as a sacrament of the church. Although the Reformers feared abuse of the Rite of Penance for very good reasons, we have, unfortunately, never constructively addressed the underlying psychological and theological issues that cry out for a place in the life of the church. There is a sense in which we do not encounter forgiveness until we face ourselves honestly and stop our games of rationalization and blaming. We devise all sorts of euphemisms for sin. We call sin mistakes, lapses, failures, shortcomings, idiosyncrasies, or character flaws.

What we *reveal*, God *heals*. What we *hide*, we are *left with*. In Gestalt psychology this process is called "owning." Our fear fragments our personality. We decide some things about us are acceptable and some things are unacceptable. Then we try to cover our unacceptabilities. But, until we own our sin and admit how intrinsic it is to our whole being, it has a destructive power. Like an undiagnosed cancer it eats away at us. We become hidden, isolated, angry at ourselves and at God. In short, we self-destruct. But when we take the roof off our lives and begin to live in the light (see I John) we discover that God can be trusted. God "is faithful and just to forgive us our sins, and to cleanse us from all unrighteousness." As long as we hide and pretend, we will never be healed. Grace cannot be denied, but it can be thwarted.

This procedure can be called confessing or it can be called owning. It can be performed in a quiet moment of prayerful reflection, performed in a group of fellow strugglers, performed in individual counseling, or performed in a corporate prayer that we claim as our own during worship, but until we reveal ourselves and start living with the roof off our lives, we will remain lonely, alienated, and untouched by grace. If we are willing, justifying grace can produce a radical continuity between our inner and outer selves, resulting in wholeness of life.

I must admit that it is much easier for me to write about this and to preach about it than it is for me to live it as a daily reality. All my life I have tried to earn my own way, to dress up my life with the trappings of piety, to acquire a sense of self-worth by achieving and succeeding. The harder I have tried, the more I have felt trapped by it all, and each new success has only deepened my feelings of failure. As a minister I expend a lot of energy earning people's love. Preach brilliant sermons so they will all line up and tell me how much they "enjoy" these little homiletical gems. Serve a bigger church, so each time I drive by it on the boulevard I can feel reassured by my prestige. Acquire more degrees. Work longer and harder than anyone else. Preach on nationwide television so everyone can see just how insightful and clever I am. Before long it all becomes one long moment of desperation, a search for blessing that goes nowhere, like a journey on a treadmill. And inside my secret skin, I always feel like an impostor, like a consummate actor playing the role of a lifetime, and it takes so much energy to keep the role intact that there is not much time to be real.

There came a point at which I had to admit that the real reason I entered the ministry was to justify myself, to cloak myself in the garments of priestliness. One would think that having served as a United States Marine and achieving a measure of success as a corporate executive, becoming a minister would free me to discover God in a more liberating way. Unfortunately, it became an ecclesiastical prison, one more way of feeling unworthy and ashamed.

For years I acted a role with my parishioners and isolated myself from other clergy. In my arrogance I told myself that it was because other preachers resented my successes. I secretly sneered that mediocrity might be contagious so why take chances on catching the disease? But deep down I knew why I couldn't form good peer relationships; it was because I always carried the fear that somehow these other ministers were real and I wasn't. I projected onto other clergy the qualities I did not believe I possessed, and assumed that they did. I imagined that they looked and acted holier than I could ever be, and I internalized a terrible pressure from lay persons to be holier than average. Arrogance and distance were just coping mechanisms for my deep-seated feelings of fear and inferiority.

Then my marriage failed. Not all at once in a fiery explosion of rage, but slowly, as a cool distance grew into an arctic separation. Someone who had loved me for a long time was suddenly no longer a part of my life. Reva was at the airport with tears in her eyes when I boarded the plane for Vietnam. She didn't bat an eye when we sold our new house to enter the ministry. She packed boxes for too many moves, counted nickels in low-paying churches, had babies with me, and finally when we couldn't bear the pain any longer we gave each other the only gift we had left, our freedom.

The more I honestly examined the reasons for the divorce, the more I realized that intimacy with me was impossible, I was too hidden. Although I understood the words of my faith, the reality of acceptance was a foreign language, and intimacy cannot truly occur without self-acceptance. After a long period of therapy and struggle, there came the day Reva and I announced the divorce to our church, and it was one of the most frightening days of my life. Suddenly there was no chance to pretend. I had failed, miserably and publicly. There was no room for pretension or excuse.

One night I found myself sitting in the living room of my district superintendent. Since our church serves as a kind of home base for him when his official duties do not take him elsewhere, I told myself I was dropping by for a pastoral visit. Suddenly I began to sob uncontrollably. All my fears of rejection and failure began to pour out like a river of bile. More than anything, I wanted him to reassure me that everything would be all right. Wisely, he refused me cheap grace, offering me instead the sacrament of his presence and his silence. After a while he said, "I don't know what will happen, but I do know that God never lets go of us. And I believe that failure sometimes opens new doors of awareness."

During this same period of time, I went away to a monastery in the California high desert. I knew that I was at a turning point, and I must either discover new reserves of strength and direction or leave the ministry. I was sick and crazy inside, close to breaking. The first several days I felt terribly out of place, frightened, and nervous, with my pathosis boiling around inside like a witch's brew in my stomach. Then after an awkward time of settling into the monkish routine of prayer, praise, and silence, generously seasoned with simplicity, I began to feel caught up in the flow of worship and contemplation. I asked for and received a confessor, who helped me wrestle with my fears and advised me to stop struggling and just listen to what God might be saying to me. One afternoon I tramped into my room, with snow on my boots, a stinging briskness on my face, and a quietness in my soul that seemed ready and receptive. Have you ever sensed the stillness of a moment when mystery surrounds you like a fresh, clean snowfall, and God seems very close? I wrote in my journal: "Outside my window, melting snow drips from the roof like moments in time slowly passing. Here time is not an enemy to be conquered or an empty vessel to be filled, it is a treasure to be savored and each moment seems exactly right, symmetrical and seamless."

Later that same night one of the monks said, "It is more important to do what is good than to do what is perfect." It was after midnight and I was sitting in front of a blazing fireplace, alone. The monk was across the room in conversation with someone else. I felt like Augustine dozing off in his garden, overhearing a conversation and taking it as his truth. "It is more important to do what is good than to do what is perfect." It struck me with the power of personal truth.

I went back to my room and after a long while, wrote in my journal:

> It became increasingly apparent to me that while I expend great energy to achieve, lead, posture, pretend and advance, I seldom consider just doing what is good. Such a simple word: good. It saddens me to think that I might achieve all my ambitions, but leave nothing behind me that is simply good. The greatest of my sins may very well be a willingness to sacrifice what is good to achieve what is admirable, perhaps I lose what is real because I expect perfection.

It wasn't an experience of dramatic conversion; I just discovered that the self-destructive games I had been playing were unnecessary. Isolation and pretension were my choices, and they were destroying any chance I would ever have to discover the joy of being accepted. I found myself singing the words of an old hymn that bubbled out like a song of praise rather than a dirge, as I had always heard it sung: "Just as I am, without one plea." I realized that if who I was in that moment, and who I am in this moment, is not enough, nothing will ever be enough, because who I am is all I have to work with. It ain't perfect, but it's enough; it ain't complete, but it's whole. It feels like being made right, it feels like justification, it feels like grace.

I fully expected my church to rise up and point an accusing finger of rejection and disgust. Instead they expressed love and concern, tried not to take sides, and although some of them undoubtedly didn't like the idea of their pastor being divorced, they supported me and my family, prayed for us, wrote notes of affirmation, and in a million small, quiet ways pastored me.

The truth is, I am only just now, barely, sometimes, once in a while, discovering what it means to be justified and accepted, to know that even though I fail myself, fail the people I love, the church I serve, and the God I speak about in such glib tones from my lofty perch above the pews, even though I am nobody's idea of what a minister ought to be, somehow; oh, blessed reality—I am acceptable. Not because of anything I have done, but because of what God has done for me in Christ.

When we encounter the God whose justifying grace accepts us, and we learn to accept that acceptance, our journey of faith becomes filled with the excitement of self-discovery. Sham and pretension are unnecessary illusions, because grace is real. If it is true that God accepts us, then it becomes possible for us to accept ourselves. Intimacy and freedom are the gifts of God's grace.

I would not normally be willing to quote *The Living Bible* publicly, since, ahem, it is a paraphrase. But there is a passage in Romans 5 that excites me, and even if it isn't accurate, it is nonetheless true:

> So now, since we have been made right in God's sight by faith in his promises, we can have real peace with him because of what Jesus Christ our Lord has done for us. For because of our faith, he has brought us into this place of highest privilege where we now stand, and we confidently and joyfully look forward to actually becoming all that God has had in mind for us to be. (Romans 5:1-2 *TLB*)

Chapter Three

Grace to Grow

One of the most sacred of my Sabbath Day activities is my afternoon nap. I usually get up well before the sun, grumble my way through coffee and the sermon outline, then dash off to church to confront the unnerving tasks of candles that will not stay lighted; microphones with loose connections (why can't someone manufacture a Methodist microphone?); last-minute liturgical adjustments; and people who confront me with an array of needs, requests, questions, complaints, and demands.

Sunday at 1:00 P.M. I remind my children that the eleventh commandment is: "Six days shalt thou labor, but on the seventh afternoon thou shalt *nap*." Thankfully none of them reads Hebrew, so I am able to carry it off. If challenged I would simply maintain that it is a textual variation found in very reliable manuscripts that were part of the Dead Sea Scrolls collection. Fatigue brings out the con man in me.

Normally my family accedes to tradition and leaves me undisturbed for a reasonable period of time.

Justin, the youngest, has always fancied himself to be above the law and tradition. One afternoon the little outlaw crept into my room and suddenly my nap was interrupted by a small hand gently, but persistently, shaking me awake.

I sat up and said, "What is it Justin?" At least, that's all I said that's fit to print.

Justin took my hands and placed them on his shoulders, without saying a word, and looked at me very expectantly. After waiting for a second, I took my hands down and once again asked, "What is it Justin?"

Without answering, he insistently took my hands and, placing them on his shoulders, looked at me very intently, as if waiting for an appropriate response. Whatever anger I felt at being awakened drained away at the look in his eyes. After several more seconds of silence, I took away my hands and asked again, "What is it Justin?"

For the third time he patiently, but wordlessly, took my hands and placed them on his shoulders, then looked me directly in the eyes and waited in silent expectation. I tried to imagine what he wanted, since it was clear that I was missing the point. So again I asked, "What is it, kid?" but this time I left my hands on his arms.

With a look of unimaginable satisfaction, Justin said, "Can't you feel me growing?" I fancied that I did feel a tremor or two.

When children are growing, even if we can't feel it happening, we can at least see the evidences of growth. Trousers, shoes, and shirts that don't fit them anymore. Inches added to their height. Appetites that overwhelm the family food budget and threaten to sink it. Even if you can't see signs of their growth every day, periodically you look at that child and think, with a strange mixture of joy and regret, "You're growing up." All parents know the special joy and mystery of watching their children change as they become first toddlers, then little boys and girls, youth, teenagers, young men and women, then adult, fully formed persons. There is regret also, because it is tempting to want to keep them close to us and dependent on us. The essence of parental love, however, is our willingness to give our children the freedom to grow.

One of the dominant biblical analogies used to describe God's relationship to us is that of a parent. Certainly, when we talk about the grace of God in any depth we see parental love, in its best sense, at work. Like any good parent, God gives us the freedom to grow, even when growth is a painful process filled with mistakes and failures.

We have already seen that, in prevenient grace, God's love comes to us first, before we even know of it or respond to it. In justifying grace we find that God through Jesus Christ has made provision to redeem us, to restore a right relationship, to forgive us, to accept us, to make us whole. Now we need to affirm also that growth is an integral part of our spiritual development. This process is associated with grace that we call sanctifying grace.

Sanctification is the progressive realization of the image of God within us. Each of us is created in God's image, something so deeply stamped within our souls that even when it is defaced or marred by the ugly depths to which human beings may sink, it is never entirely eradicated. The likeness that exists between God and God's children is the basis for our growth and development. Sanctifying grace is the freedom and the strength that we receive as we try to become all that God has in mind for us to be.

There are four important aspects of sanctifying grace that we want to examine here: (1) It does not happen all at once; therefore, it requires patience. (2) Because it is a gradual process, it must take into account our human capacity for mistakes and sinfulness. (3) It is not simply individualistic, but is best understood within a community of faith where formation is taken seriously. (4) Ultimately, it compels us beyond ourselves to mission in the world.

1. Be Patient

It is important to note that just as we do not grow from infant to adult in one week, neither should we expect our spiritual development to be sudden. It takes time, patience, and lots and lots of grace.

Several years ago I lost fifty pounds. Most of my life I have been slim, but over a period of six years while I worked on graduate degrees and tried to support a family at the same time, a weight problem crept up on me. No exercise and late-night meals added excess pounds to a body that couldn't take them gracefully.

There came a day when I looked at myself in the mirror and said, "Yuck." As I began dieting and exercising, I joined a health club. You can't be an authentic Californian (which some people consider an oxymoron) without joining a health club. All new members were assigned a personal fitness consultant. Mine turned out to be a disgusting specimen of physical legerdemain whose neat little gym suit bulged in all the right places and displayed his well-formed body to its best advantage. I hated him on sight. He looked me over, new shoes, new shirt, new shorts, and said, "Just getting started, huh? Let's see what you can do." We went from weight machines to jogging track to scales in a very short amount of time. At the end of each paltry effort on my part, he would glance up from his clipboard with ill-disguised contempt and ask, "Is that all?" Finally I put him in his place by saying, between gasps of breath, "I used to be a Marine." He looked up in surprise and said, "Goes to show you it can happen to anybody." As we went to record my beginning body weight so we could measure progress, I asked, hopefully, "How long will it take me to lose fifty pounds?" Without skipping a beat, or even looking up from the clipboard, he asked, "How long did it take you to get this way?"

We are, of course, an impatient people. Instant gratification has become a watchword of this society. Instant cameras develop the picture right before our eyes. Banks now have twenty-four-hour ready-teller machines so we can withdraw our cash at any time, with no delay. In fact, on one occasion when I was fussing at my boys about putting more money in their piggy banks, Benjamin suggested that we just install one of the "bank machines" in their bedroom, so they could put their quarters in and get out twenty-dollar bills. I had to explain to him that I didn't just take money out of the machine any time I wanted it, as he seemed to think. There was also something called a deposit.

Our supermarket shelves are filled with instant foods ranging from soup and coffee to complicated precooked meals that our microwave ovens can prepare in just minutes. Someone said they overheard one mother rebuking her son in the grocery store, saying, "Put that back. It has to be cooked."

We don't even wait for all the votes to be counted in our presidential elections. NBC, CBS, and ABC will announce the winner of an election with only 2 percent of the vote counted. During the last election a President was "elected" before I could get to the California polls to vote against him.

In fact, believe it or not, you can even become an instant martyr according to an article I recently clipped. You can send away for a framable award that reads,

> The suffering you have had to endure at the hands of life has been almost more than any person can bear. Rarely has such a noble soul been forced to put up with such undeserved agony. In recognition of your extraordinary plight, the Church of World Peace hereby awards this Certificate of Martyrdom.

Just mail five dollars and a letter listing three tragic events in your life to the church in Denver, Colorado, and become an instant martyr. The organization says it offers the award to those who find it difficult to get through their day and need something "to console their misery."

What we get too easily, and reach too quickly, we esteem too lightly. Spiritual growth is not a quick process. We won't get there tomorrow. Every life needs testing, training, and forming mixed into the process of failing and succeeding to achieve growth in God's grace. Usually we live in a time of "inbetween-ness." I know that's not good English, but it is descriptive of sanctification, when the Holy Spirit is guiding us and forming us into God's image.

To encounter the power of Christ that justifies us is an incredible experience. But it isn't the end of grace. Not by a long shot. Grace is at work throughout our lives. Sometimes in fact, we may discover that not only in our higher, finer, spiritual moments, but also in those moments when we fail in dreadful, dis-couraging ways, we are being sanctified. These heights and depths are the range of grace in all its fullness.

I have known people who just looked and acted like saints, and frankly it can be discouraging, because nobody would describe me as saintly. Some people are better by nature than others are by grace, although it is important not to confuse holiness with a low metabolic rate. Many of us have many shortcomings, and our lives are filled with miserable episodes of failing and falling short of our Christian ideals. We say awful things, act impulsively, make the wrong decisions, hurt the people we love. We need to be reminded that holiness is possible, but our journey toward it does require patience.

2. *Make Friends of Your Failures*

A seeker after truth came to a saint for guidance.
"Tell me please, wise one, how did you become holy?"
"Two words."
"And what are they, please?"
"Right choices."
"And how does one learn to choose correctly?"
"One word."
"May I know it, please?"
"Growth."
"How does one grow?"
"Two words."
"What are those words, pray tell me?"
"Wrong choices."
When you and I begin our journey into wholeness and holiness, we must go through the frustration of failing and making wrong choices. Spiritual development does not unfold like an ever-ascending escalator. It is marked by peaks and valleys. Although we affirm that we are created in the image of God, we are also created as free persons, with the potential to choose between right and wrong. This potential for choice provides the opportunity for sinful or less-than-moral activity. But, our transgressions are also the occasions for deepened understandings of how Christ is at work in our lives. In spiritually healthy persons, making the wrong choice can result in a holy guilt that becomes

productive in rethinking and moving to a higher understanding of the Christian experience.

The goal of sanctification is the internalization of God's law. The Bible calls this having the law "written in our hearts." As this occurs, we begin to see that we sin not only against God, but also against ourselves. We are the ones who are thwarted and diminished. We are the ones who become less than we could be, less than we want to be, less than our own best selves. If we aspire to the sanctified heights of holy living we will do well to find footholds in those places where we struggle with our sinfulness and our failure.

Poor Richard says, "Experience keeps a dear school, but fools will learn in no other." We must all be fools then, because nothing teaches us more quickly than our own experience. Have you ever walked up to an elevator where a crowd of people have gathered to wait? Most of us may notice that the call light for up or down has been pressed. But watch how many people will go ahead and press the light anyway. We just don't believe the elevator will come unless we push the light. Or, try telling a child that the eye of a stove is hot. You say "Hot!" in a loud voice. The child knows you said hot! and may even know what hot is. But watch how often that small hand must venture toward the source of heat. The child thinks, "He said hot. But what does he know about hot? This may only be lukewarm." Experience is a good teacher.

Someone once encouraged Abraham Lincoln to destroy his enemies. He is said to have replied, "Don't I destroy them when I make them my friends?" We make friends with our failures when we allow them to become our teachers and our guides.

3. We Can't Do It Alone

Sanctification is not a process that the individual engages in alone. We are in a "company of saints," a community of people who seek spiritual transformation. The church is at its best when it becomes a community of moral and spiritual formation, where we may speak to one another heart to heart, and move beyond our individualistic boundaries into the fullness of hearing one another's stories and becoming teachers to one another as those who journey together. Unfortunately, we have not taken this as seriously as we should. It requires resolve on our part, and discipline, and a willingness to be open to one another, to put aside our isolation and our plastic theology. In short, this community begins when we become human to one another, vulnerable to one another, and available to one another, to the world, and to the presence of the Holy Spirit in the world.

Certainly one of the places we should encounter one another with honesty and vulnerability is in our church life. But, too often we have allowed the church to become a place for casual association. Our churches have an abundance of committees and boards, but few occasions where real transformation can take place. Although it is true that we gather regularly for worship, and though it can also be argued that one of the purposes of worship is spiritual growth in grace, there is not enough room within the hour of worship for us to fully discover a sanctified life.

In the early stages of Methodism's development, this purpose was served by the Class Meeting, and in fact, formal worship was not even a part of early Methodism's emergence, since the adherents were still Anglicans. The gradual disappearance of the Class Meeting produced a vacuum of opportunity for sanctifying grace to take shape in our members' lives. In these Class Meetings, there was room for self-examination, confession, study, questioning, and guiding. Most important, a commitment to ideas and works beyond an individual's narrow self-interests emerged from these meetings.

It is not within the scope of this work to analyze this problem in any depth. But excellent resources are available for people who want to take the problem seriously. Covenant Discipleship groups are one way many of us have found to recapture this vital dimension of Christian experience. You can find out more about Covenant Discipleship groups by writing to: Discipleship Resources, P. O. Box 840, Nashville, TN 37202. I commend them to you. There are, of course, other ways of discovering community and guidance. Spiritual directors are available in many places but should be chosen carefully. Bible study can become a means of holy living when it incorporates other disciplines, such as keeping a journal, honest self-examination and disclosure, and a struggle for mission commitments.

4. *Sanctification and Liberation*

The constant struggle of the Christian faith, and every one of us who tries to live it, is the struggle to find ourselves, yet lose ourselves. Remember Simeon Stylites, one of the early Christians? He is famous for spending year after year sitting on top of a sixty-foot column, even before the *Guinness Book of World Records* was around to encourage this kind of behavior. He apparently believed that this was a denial of self that fulfilled Jesus' teaching. We can commend him for at least acknowledging that it would take time to become a holy person. But if you think about it for a moment, a person must be very self-centered to spend thirty years sitting on top of a column in the interest of self-denial.

Christians have fasted to the point of death, worn hair shirts, and even abstained from sex in order to deny themselves. Usually, however, we just end up self-centered in a different way.

It reminds me of the dilemma of the child who was given a new boomerang for a birthday present and became frustrated because the old one couldn't be thrown away. Victor Frankl wrote,

> While I was lecturing in Melbourne, Australia, some years ago, I was given a boomerang as a souvenir gift. In contemplating this gift, I concluded that in a sense it symbolized human existence. One generally assumes that a boomerang returns to the thrower. Actually it returns only when the thrower has missed the target. Similarly a person returns to self, to be concerned with self, only after missing the mission, only after failing to find the meaning of life.

Jesus did not say, "Deny yourself." He said, "Deny yourself . . . Follow me . . . Whoever loses his life for my sake shall find it." It is here, of course, that the Me Generation cries, "Stop. I want to get off." To find life by losing it for Christ's sake is not a sudden transaction. If you're looking for instant satisfaction, instant relationships, instant love, instant money, or instant achievement, they won't be found in the bargain that Jesus offers. What we are offered is a meaning for life that will not boomerang. True self-fulfillment, in light of sanctifying grace, is to be found in following Jesus as servants of love, generosity, justice, and mercy in behalf of the whole world.

I am no expert in Liberation Theology, but I know enough to be appalled at how seldom the church in this country has really listened to its message. We cannot naively believe that our self-centered brand of religion will bring us the power of transformed lives and a transformed world. We own too much, live too much to ourselves, seek our own way, and entrench ourselves behind a narrow brand of piety. Where have we denied ourselves and truly taken up the cross to follow Jesus into this world of pain, poverty, and injustice? Why do the church's priorities continue to reflect essentially idolatrous self-interest? Why do we cling to our concern with administrative orders rather than effective mission in the world? How can we speak of evangelism when we are the ones in need of the gospel message?

Dag Hammarskjöld has written, "In our time, the road to holiness leads through the world of action." Sanctifying grace must always compel us beyond ourselves to a radical reordering of our lives and our priorities. Then and only then do we become "vessels fit for God's service."

A Parable

Once upon a time when the world was very young, shortly after Adam and Eve had been expelled from the ease of paradise, they wandered the face of the earth trying to find a place of hospitality and belonging. Each night, at first, they wept for all that they had lost, and despaired of ever finding a home.

Some of the places they discovered were too rocky and desolate. Some of the land was too swampy and moist. Some places were too high, some too low. Some places were desert and some were arctic.

Finally they found a stretch of ground with trees to break the heat of the day, water to irrigate the land, and soaring mountains to capture their imagination. They settled here. Adam began to till the land and grow their food with the sweat of his brow. Often Eve worked beside him in the fields. Soon they turned a cave into a home. Children came from the union of their flesh, and the world was quickly populated with many peoples. Adam and Eve were venerated in their old age, always hospitable to strangers, whom they knew to be flesh of their flesh. They accumulated neither too much nor too little, and wanted nothing they did not need.

One evening after Adam and Eve had finished a long day and tucked the great grandchildren away for the night, they were sitting together on the ledge outside their home, watching as the sun said its daily good-bye behind the glorious mountains. After a while, Adam turned and said: "Eve, God was wrong. We were never meant to live in a paradise where everything was given to us without toil, where there was no heaven to gain and no hell to avoid. God was wrong. This is the way we were meant to live, where we struggle and bleed, where we must find out for ourselves what is just and what is not, where we must reason and strive, where we must gain and lose, live and die. This is how a human should live."

He became so overwhelmed by the thought that he stood to his feet in the twilight and shook his fist toward heaven. In his loudest voice he shouted, "God you were wrong!"

And somewhere, so far away your mind cannot conceive of the distance, but so close the breath of the man was hot upon God's cheek—God smiled.

Chapter Four

Strong at the Broken Places

Early that week, excitement began to grow in our house. Each morning at breakfast we ate cereals, anticipation, and milk. Each day we found time after homework to refine our hopes. Even television was cast aside as a pale shadow of our present joy and our very tangible dream.

We read the instructions again and again, endlessly discussing strategy and the finer points of engineering and aerodynamics. We were quite a sight. It was the week when Benjamin stopped calling himself seven and a half and insisted on being eight years old, only four months early. Justin kept asking if he could be eight, but had to settle for five years old, and never mind his June birthday. I felt about ten years old at most, but honored and healed to be a part of the project.

Benjamin insisted on wearing his new Cub Scout hat, Justin borrowed my cap that says, "American by birth, Southern by the grace of God," and I wore my old blue graduate-school cap, which has a bright patch with "Kierkegaard" on it, who was little or no help at all to us as we huddled around the table and tinkered away at our entry in the Cub Scouts' Pinewood Derby. All week long my sons and I shared the once in a lifetime pleasure of creating our very first miniature wooden race car. What was once a block of pine became a gleaming, red, streamlined automobile with low, sleek lines and plastic wheels attached with small nails.

The race was scheduled for Friday evening, so by Thursday evening I felt very confident that we had done everything humanly possible to produce a winning entry. We had cut and sanded, carefully painted, adjusted and readjusted the wheels, looked at the car from every possible angle, and heeded Justin's five-year-old wisdom that constantly called for more oil on the wheels.

As I put the boys to bed Thursday evening, they asked that the lamp be left burning and the car placed in the small pool of light so that they could wake up and look at it once in a while. *Then*, as we sat on the bed, Benjamin dropped a bomb, in his sweetest, most innocent voice. "Dad," he said, "could we pray over the car?" "Well, of course," I answered. "That would be a good idea." So they brought the car to me like trusting ushers bringing a handicapped person forward to the healing touch of Oral Roberts. I wasn't too sure about the liturgical format for a prayer over a race car, but I knew that Jesus had said, "Suffer the little children and forbid them not to bring their race cars unto me," or something like that.

There are many disadvantages to having a Dad

who's a United Methodist preacher and a notable mechanical klutz, so I was gratified that at least there was something I could do effectively and with confidence. During the prayer Benjamin was taking no chances, so he adopted a very traditional, hands-under-chin posture, as if he wanted to be sure God knew he was taking this seriously. Justin, always the observer, kept his eyes open the whole time to watch me closely as I occasionally peeked at him to see if his eyes were closed, and cocked his head as a sign of skepticism. I hope I will not seem immodest when I tell you it was one of my better prayers, including gratitude for the love we shared, joy at our opportunity to be partners in God's creative process, and intercession for the stability of the plastic wheels, which had by now slightly deteriorated from the interaction of the plastic and Justin's daily anointing with oil.

As I finished, and waited to see if there was anything the boys wanted to add, Benjamin opened one eye and softly said, "Dad, you didn't pray for me to win." It is no exaggeration when I tell you that that one hit me right between the eyes. I said, "Time out guys." In case you didn't know, dear readers, "time out" is the ancient Coptic formulation occasionally used between "Our Father" and "Amen" to signify a pause for roundtable discussion. It lets God know that we're going to take a short break and God can listen to someone else for a minute, God having many prayers to be heard.

I stumbled my way through an explanation of why I couldn't pray for our car to win, including problems inherent in traditional notions of prayer and their relationship to God's omnipotence, neatly summarizing the contributions of Liberation Theology, Wittgenstein's impact on the history of philosophy, John Hicks' interpretation of eschatological verification, and concluding with a few cogent observations about a process view of prayer. Benjamin was on the verge of reductionist tears as he said, "You mean you won't pray for me to win." I promised myself a long time ago never to pray for divine influence on the outcome of football games or conflict between nations. "But how," I muttered under my breath, "can I refuse to ask God's help for Benjamin's car to win the race?" What kind of father wouldn't ask his Boss to grant a small favor for his son?

Theology having failed to get the point across, I tried a Knute Rockne approach, in which I endeavored to praise the importance of trying our best and pointed out to Benjamin that winning wasn't the point, that doing our best should always be our goal. He countered with a version of Bill Veeck's heresy, Winning isn't everything; it's the only thing.

Finally we compromised on a prayer that used the time-honored hedge, "If it be thy will, allow our car to win." Benjamin took over from me, praying a lusty, all-stops-out prayer for final and ultimate victory. Justin stayed out of it except for one final "Let's put more oil on the wheels," and they went to bed, if not to sleep, perchance to dream.

Friday evening finally arrived. Before the Toyota van even stopped rolling, we piled out and calmly swaggered into the John Burroughs School auditorium, with Benjamin in the lead, looking every bit of eight years old in his new Cub Scout blue shirt with Pack 175 patch and the American flag over the right-hand pocket. We held hands in a lapse of manliness and entered a packed room that fairly throbbed with energy and excitement.

I knew we were in trouble right from the start. It became quickly apparent that there were what looked like hundreds of very capable, very intense fathers and sons. I knew just how Lee Iacocca must feel when I realized with heart-stopping fear that quite a few of them were Japanese. My Kierkegaard cap never felt more out of place than in the moment I approached the race track and realized I was standing beside a father-son team who wore matching Ferrari jackets. These people were taking this very seriously. *And their cars* . . . I can't begin to tell you. We had simply painted ours red and gummed on the numeral 3 to represent Daddy, Benjamin, and Justin or Father, Son, and Holy Terror, I can't remember which. But some of these cars did not look like the product of eight-year-old hands assisted by fatherly wisdom. They looked like something out of *Road and Track* magazine. Justin looked around and said, "Maybe we need more oil on the wheels." The Japanese father beside me overheard the remark and helpfully said, "Oh, no! Never use oil, it erodes the plastic. You should use graphite." I immediately resolved to trade my Toyota van first thing Monday morning.

Finally our names were called. Benjamin reached up, took my hand, and we placed our car at the top of the track, which had been ingeniously designed with a six-foot-high starting line that swooped down, roller coaster fashion, to a finish line about thirty feet away. I noticed Benjamin's other hand typically had crossed fingers. Finally, with a "Ready, Set, Go," the cars were released and seemed to fly down to the finish line, or at least some of them did. One of them, painted red, with the number three, seemed to just stroll down the incline and embarrassingly stopped two feet short of the finish line, several seconds after the winner.

Quietly running tears rolled slowly down Benjamin's cheeks, tracking their way to a finish line, and his lip began to quiver. We picked up our derby baby, which no longer looked sleek and dangerous, and walked together to our family car, soon to be traded for a Chrysler. After we got in, we sat for a moment in a silence too deep for words. Finally, Benjamin said very quietly, "I guess we should have prayed more." I was grateful he didn't scold my theology. Then Justin, from the backseat, said, "Yeah, and used gwaphite on the wheels."

You and I are often tempted to believe that God rewards the righteous and punishes sinners. How many of our own prayers have we offered petitioning God's favor on our behalf? Don't we wonder what justice can mean in a world where good people perish, while evil prospers? How often do we forget that righteousness is its own reward and sin its own worst enemy?

Occasionally we get confused on this point and try to draw direct parallels of cause and effect between goodness and success, between sin and suffering. It is easy then to erroneously conclude that if we lose or if we suffer, God is punishing us, and if we win or prosper, God is rewarding us. It is tempting to believe, as Benjamin did, that if we had only prayed more or had more faith, God would have brought things around to our desired conclusion.

Recently we have heard ministers of the gospel, who should know better, suggesting that AIDS is God's punishment for homosexuality. This kind of thinking is connected with a theology that says you wouldn't be sick if you had enough faith to be healed. One bumper sticker even goes so far as to claim "Prosperity is my divine right."

It must be admitted that there are Old Testament passages that seem to suggest a correlation between sin and sickness, between righteousness and prosperity, and when read by themselves these biblical passages would lead us to conclude that all you have to do is pray, or lead a righteous life, and God will heap abundance and blessing on you.

To see the problem from this point of view, we need only remind ourselves that many good people suffer, and drawing cause-and-effect conclusions between prosperity and righteousness is contrary to the gospel. If you look closely you will see that Jesus teaches us that even if the tower of Siloam falls on people, or the plague destroys human life, or suffering and poverty cripple human existence, or if misfortune strikes suddenly, it is no indication of our righteousness or lack thereof. In other words, it's just that kind of world folks, and maybe Justin was right after all: It has something to do with graphite and engineering design, and less to do with who prays the longest, or is most deserving.

Paul assures us that "suffering produces endurance, and endurance produces character, and character produces hope, and hope does not disappoint us, because God's love has been poured into our hearts through the Holy Spirit which has been given to us" (Rom. 5:3-5 RSV). I can't explain the mystery of suffering, or clarify the nature of evil. But like Paul, I believe that somehow grace permeates the process, and if, even tentatively, grace can become connected with our suffering, then strangely enough our suffering becomes more bearable.

Victor Frankl was a Jewish prisoner of war in one of Hitler's concentration camps during World War II. Out of that experience he wrote a book called *Man's Search for Meaning.* Frankl noted that "suffering ceases to be suffering in some way the moment it finds meaning." What meaning can we find in our suffering? What purpose does it serve? How can suffering be redemptive? In a grace-filled passage that opens II Corinthians, Paul says,

> Praise be to the God and Father of our Lord Jesus Christ, . . . the God of all comfort, who comforts us in all our troubles, *so that we can comfort those in any trouble with the comfort we ourselves have received from God.* . . . We were under great pressure, far beyond our ability to endure, so that we despaired even of life. Indeed, in our hearts we felt the sentence of death. *But this happened so that we might not rely on ourselves but on God, who raises the dead.* He has delivered us from such a

deadly peril . . .. On him we have set our hope that he will continue to deliver us as you help us by your prayers. Then *many will give thanks* on our behalf for the gracious favor granted us in answer to the prayers of many. (II Cor. 1:3-4, 8-11 NIV, italics mine)

So that we can comfort those in trouble with the comfort we have received

Sometimes the wounds we have received become the channels through which others are healed. There is an authenticity that comes from our suffering. No one can help like the one who can say, "I've been there."

I pastor an incredible woman who is a recovering alcoholic. I knew her when she scarcely drew a sober breath, when she hid bottles from her husband, lashed out at the people around her, blamed her problems on everybody but herself, made herself miserable in a hundred sips a day. A beautiful young woman who was slowly killing herself. She found something one day that recovering alcoholics call a "Higher Power." Today when Nancy talks about the wholeness that God brings into broken human lives, people listen. There are millions like her who belong to AA groups, meeting in church basements and other tucked-away quiet places. In their meetings they introduce themselves and admit their problem. They support one another in ways that constantly amaze me, and, I'm told, no one can help an alcoholic like someone who's been there and can say, "Through the power of God, my Higher Source, I am whole today."

It was my privilege to be a friend of an activist with

Affirmation, the United Methodist caucus of gays and lesbians. He died of AIDS so slowly and painfully it seemed it would never end. His last year was an experience many of us shall never forget. In the midst of this awful thing that happened to him he said, "I refuse to be a victim because I am a child of God." As I went in and out of his hospital room, I encountered people whose lives were being changed forever because of Lyle and the witness he gave to God's grace. I can preach a hundred sermons about grace, write book after book about it, and never come close to healing people the way Lyle did. He didn't just talk about grace, he lived it.

During the darkest times of my divorce, the people who could speak to me with the most authority were people who had come through their own divorce and found light on the other side of darkness. I don't recommend divorce to anyone, but when I try to minister to people who are suffering through it, grace is more than a theory, it's something I know about.

I watch some of the widows and widowers in our church when a husband or a wife dies. People who are of most help to these bereaved are those who themselves have known the terrible sense of loss, the wrenching process of grieving, the haunting memory of love that was shared and life that was created.

Sympathy is cheap. It costs no more than a glib card, or a quick telephone call. Empathy is expensive. It has cost us something when we've been there ourselves, found grace to get through it, and then awkwardly give what we ourselves have already been given.

Just as we affirm that by the wounds of Jesus we

have been healed, we affirm also that our wounds have the potential to become grace for others.

So that we might not rely on ourselves but on God

The idolatry of self-sufficiency ends quickly in the face of great suffering. One of my closest friends is a highly successful lawyer, a partner in one of the largest law firms in Los Angeles. He is considered a brilliant attorney. He has a beautiful wife, two lovely children, lives in a stately home, and he's barely forty. If you met him today you would walk away impressed with the depth of his spirituality. He knows more Thomas Merton than just about anybody I know. When our church elected him lay leader he came to me and said: "I'm not interested in telling you how to run the church. That doesn't interest me. Frankly, I don't have time for church politics. I am much more interested in leading a life of prayer and calling the church to new depths of renewal and commitment." Now friends, I know a few pastors who would trade their Ph.D. for a lay leader like that. He begins each day in his office high above the city, sitting quietly at his desk in prayer, and when he has to make major decisions he prays about them. There have been a few things he and I differ on, but I am constantly amazed at how this very successful man acknowledges a divine power at work in his life.

Fred would tell you that he relies on God and God alone to find out what is real and what is illusion. He gives away a substantial portion of the money he earns to acknowledge God's goodness and blessing. Know how he got this way? He totaled his nice coupe one day. Almost killed himself. Broke his back. Wore a full body cast like an excruciating suit of armor. And while the healing was taking place, when he had nothing better to do, he began to realize how fragile his pretensions to self-sufficiency were. He began to read the Bible. He had been the president of his Methodist Youth Fellowship when he was a teenager, but he had long since left that behind. His accident had the effect of opening his life once more to the presence of God. Near death brought him new life. In pain he found strength and an abundance of grace. At the end of himself, he found God.

We learn to give thanks

The third grace-filled meaning that Paul finds in suffering is this: We learn to give thanks. I am not certain that even now I know very much about this business of learning to be thankful for the right stuff. It's easy to be grateful for things that we enjoy. It is somewhat more difficult to embrace our fear, our sadness, our failure, our doubt, our pain, and somehow be thankful that God mixes them in with joy, pleasure, and success.

One month and one day after my fortieth birthday, I came home from a very long, very stressful day, in a long, stressful week of an interminable, stressful year, sat down for a moment in the silence of my bedroom to catch my breath, and found out that I couldn't. My chest felt as if an elephant was sitting on it; I started

67

sweating, the pain started spreading into my right shoulder, and I thought, "This is silly. I can't be having a heart attack."

I sat there for a few minutes, telling myself how silly it was, while the pain got worse. I could see myself going to the hospital, sitting in the emergency room, with people around me who were really sick, and then the doctor walking in saying, "Look stupid, it's just something you ate" (which, as it turned out, was at least partially true).

When the pain wouldn't go away, I called my good friend Susan who lives next door and said, "I know this sounds dumb, but would you drive me to the hospital; I'm having chest pains." All the way to the hospital I kept saying, "This is silly, I'm not having a heart attack." She kept saying, "Fine, you can feel foolish at the hospital."

Within minutes they hooked me up to tubes, oxygen, and an EKG machine, while I felt sillier and sillier about the whole process, until the doctor walked in and said, "You're having a heart attack." That tended to get my attention.

Over the next few hours as my children came in for a few moments, we held on to one another through our tears and our prayers. I don't think I've ever wanted life any more than I wanted it in those moments, not just for myself, but for them. I wanted to see them grow up. I wanted to hold their children in my arms and find out about being a grandparent. Memories flooded my mind. Why had I let so many other things be more important than these three little persons I loved more than anything in the whole world.

When the children left, my best friend Mark came in, and that was the hardest moment of all, because we had to talk about what to do if . . . and you don't even want to finish the thought.

Now, some months after those awful, painful, frightening moments, I have a different perspective on my life. I want to be careful how I say this to you, but here it is: I'm thankful this happened to me. I wasn't feeling grateful at the time, and I would have been quite upset at anyone's glibly suggesting to me in the emergency room of Cedars-Sinai Hospital that I ought to be thankful for a heart attack. But with the passing of time, I am learning to be thankful. Flowers, cards, phone calls, all the usual list of things to be thankful for. I can still jog, play golf, exercise, and the list goes on. But more than that there is, I think, a renewed sense of what is important and what isn't. What I want and what I don't want. What prices I am willing to pay and what isn't worth the cost. In short, an awful moment of suffering and fear has become a source of gratitude and grace.

My mother used to say, "Be careful what you pray for. You might get it." I'm coming to realize how profound that really is. Be careful when you pray for courage. It can only be found in moments of fear. Strength comes from being tested. Wisdom comes from perplexity. All of these sought-after qualities do not come cheap. God hews them from the brokenness and struggle of our lives. Sometimes we learn to be grateful for the strangest, most surprising things, because we find that grace emerges from them like a butterfly from its cocoon.

Chapter Five

Lord of the Ordinary

Some of my most cherished childhood memories grew out of our annual campmeetings. We had a beautiful, rustic district campground tucked away in the Carolina woods. It had a lake where snakes occasionally swam with us, and frogs gathered on warm evenings to croak their Hallelujah chorus while the alto cricket section kept time.

Beside the lake was a tabernacle with a rusted tin roof, open sides, and sawdust on the floor. When it rained, even the most resonant-voiced evangelists had trouble being heard above the clatter. Not that we listened to them much anyway. Mostly the kids sat along the very back on rough, unfinished benches that could slip a splinter right through the seat of your blue jeans and leave you squirming in agony while all the other little boys giggled, saying, "Don't look at me, I ain't pulling no splinter out of there."

Almost every service had something surprising and unpredictable. I remember one service with guest singers Billy and Wanda Braxton. They traveled around in an old bus, with "Billy and Wanda" painted on the sides. Since it was summertime they had brought along their kids. During the service, while Billy and Wanda were singing, the children were expected to sit on the front pew and behave themselves as an example to the young sinners chewing gum along the back benches.

Billy and Wanda's children, unfortunately, proved to be unwilling examples. They clowned and frolicked without taking any notice of their frustrated parents, who, trapped on the platform, continually tried to get the children's attention by snapping their fingers and contorting their eyes, mouth, and nose into unique facial expressions that went largely unnoticed by the Braxton kids, but that were noticed by the rest of us with infinite amusement.

Billy and Wanda were trapped because they were being paid to sing gospel songs as they accompanied themselves on guitar and piano. But the moment of truth, which we sinners in the back had eagerly anticipated, finally arrived. When they finished the evening's songs, Billy stormed off the platform, paused by the scene of turmoil just long enough to throw his four-year-old son across his shoulder, and started down the aisle toward the back. Everyone in the tabernacle, including the four-year-old boy, knew that a spanking waited in the darkness out of sight and beyond hearing from the tin-roofed tabernacle.

Just as Billy passed by the sinners' seat in the back, the lad, who was folded in half across his dad's shoulder and bouncing with every step, put his little hands in the small of his dad's back, pushed himself up, and in a voice that was loud enough for all to hear said, "Ya'll pray for me now, hear."

You and I are not so different from that boy. We all tend to be very religious in times of crisis, but most of the time we just go it alone. For many people God is present only in times of trouble. This is called foxhole faith, from the statement of the Reverend William Cummings during World War II that "there are no atheists in foxholes." I suspect that when the Gallup polls inform us that a large percentage of the American people pray, it may be this kind of prayer.

Isn't it true that many of us expect to encounter God only during worship in a church or synagogue? Millions of people show up each Sunday morning, dressed in their Sunday best, quietly enter the sanctuary, and act very subdued for an hour or so, because after all, in a place of worship one is in the presence of Almighty God.

For these people church is something apart from the rest of the world, and it has its own time, place, code of conduct, rituals, and language. They come to church to find a sense of God's presence, and, one suspects, they go back home presuming the requirements of faith have been fulfilled for another week. Any business God has with these people should be transacted, they seem to believe, between 10:30 and 11:30 on Sunday morning.

The result of this mindset is a service of worship that exists wholly apart from whatever happens during the other 167 hours of the week. This variety of faith requires a vocabulary of its own, the meaning of which is not always readily apparent. If we are not very careful, liturgy can launder the color out of worship and leave us with a neatly pressed, but lifeless one-hour martinized experience.

Too often, our only sense of God's presence is confined to this weekly dose of the sacred, when we are inoculated with a shot of divinity and sent forth into our very secular existence, which seems unrelated to worship and faith.

Someone has suggested that, for many of us, religion is like an artificial limb. It has neither warmth nor life, and though it helps us stumble along, it never becomes a part of us. We strap it on once a week and take it off after Sunday lunch to limp through the ordinary demands of daily living.

After finding so little of God throughout the week, it is no wonder we find so little of God's presence in worship.

I am perfectly willing to admit that some of the blame for this tragedy should be placed upon the silk-yoked shoulders of the clergy. It seems that we are forever dreaming up even more abstract and obtuse catchwords to trade with one another, like cherished theological baseball cards. "I'll trade you one apocalyptic eschatology for one ground of ultimate being." "No, how about two apocalyptic eschatologies for one get-out-of-hell-free card."

In part this is because we spent a lot of years and borrowed unreasonable sums of money to finance our seminary degrees, and now, bless the Lord, we learned Greek, so we'll make it Greek for everybody. It seems as if the more degrees we accumulate and the longer we hang around these stained-glass houses, the harder it becomes to engage in ordinary conversation. Some days I meet someone on the street and that person says, "Hello. How are you?" I have to remind myself not to say, "And also with you."

But part of the responsibility is also to be shared by the laity. Too often, church becomes a safe harbor for those times when the winds of change are blowing the pieces of life around. So we anchor our souls in the haven of rest and sail the wild seas no more. "Don't change things" becomes the cry. Use the old familiar words, sing the comfortably quiet hymns, and let us join together as we watch the world go by. Without meaning to, we create an environment in which the uninitiated are set adrift.

It wasn't always this way. Many of the elements of worship are taken from ordinary existence. The robes worn by clergy, for example, were once the clothes of every Roman citizen. Ministerial salaries being what they are, it is natural that we can't change styles too often.

If you look closely, the symbols of faith are usually rooted in the soil of everyday life. We call the church, for example, a family of faith. Candles were not invented just to sit upon altars. Water is no less sacred when it is poured over your head in the shower than when it is poured over your head in baptism. And upon what we call the high altar sit the very basics of ordinary existence: bread and wine, the stuff of life.

Sometimes we are confused into thinking that Christianity is a spiritual religion, as if our faith is only intangible and otherworldly. Nothing could be farther from the faith as Jesus preached it.

Jesus had a way of taking the stuff of everyday life—coins, mustard seeds, daily work, water, bread, wine—and using it to help us see the presence of God in our everyday lives. By his very presence, Jesus witnessed to a God who, in God's great love, chose to use earthly, physical objects and actions to reveal God's self to us.

It isn't that I don't enjoy the liturgy or appreciate the beauty of a lovely cathedral. There have been many, many moments when the power of the church's life and language has overwhelmed me and renewed my soul. But these moments are not somehow more sacred than other moments. The whole life of the church becomes sacramental only when it points beyond itself to the power and presence of Christ in the world. The creation itself is sacred.

I was trying to make this point recently to a group of fundamentalist clergy, whose fellowship I cherish, and was taken to task rather sharply because I chose to speak on the Bible as literature. The hallmark of truly great literature is its ability to illuminate the complexity of the human situation. Small wonder, then, that the Bible should be considered one of the greatest pieces of literature ever written. Whatever else it may be, the Bible is a collection of powerful stories with unlikely, eccentric characters, who are as flawed as the rest of us, but who, somehow, manage to stumble their way through encounters with the Living God and discover the power of divine grace to transform human life from one-dimensional existence into moment after moment of surprise and mystery.

For all of us, faith must be shaped by the ordinary

events of daily life that renew our hope. Sometimes these are experiences as spectacular as the ecstasies of which William James wrote in *The Varieties of Religious Experience*. At other times, they are experiences as simple and as ordinary as the touch of a friendly hand, reconciliation after a quarrel, the smile of a stranger on the street, a fat, little kid toddling across the room, or a glorious sunrise that shimmers briefly just for us, the moon glowing on a winter lake at night, or even just the stillness of a pregnant silence.

Whatever religion we carry within us, and most of us have just enough to make us miserable, is the result of those experiences which renew our hope and give us a sense of purpose and direction in shaping the remaining moments of our life. Some of us call these experiences stories. Our stories are what makes us human. Our stories reveal the holy. Our stories connect us as a community of people who share certain imagery and are bound together by a common desperate hope.

Stories are sacraments in the best sense of the word because they bring grace to everyday moments and give it a common touch. And if just once you are surprised to find God in an ordinary moment and an ordinary place, then your whole world may become transparent. The world and its moment-by-moment existence is the transparent means by which God's face appears to us. Perhaps life itself is the truest sacrament of all, for Jesus Christ is truly Lord of the ordinary.

Chapter Six

The Unpredictability of God

Once we discover the way God's grace has been at work in our lives, it is surprising how quickly we decide who may and may not receive grace in the full measure we have been given. Religious history from Jonah to Jonestown is full of people who want to hoard grace for themselves and those like them. Fortunately, God seems to have other ideas.

I met a man recently in the Gospel of John who reminded me how God's grace appears in unlikely places and people. He was a veteran of more military campaigns than he cared to think about, with a face of indeterminate age, burned by the sun of a dozen countries, and wrinkling now in paper-fine age lines around those eyes which had seen too much during the past twenty years of loyal service to Caesar. His hair was bristly cut in the fashion preferred by military men with traces of gray showing through the hair oil. The first two fingers of his right hand were nicotine-stained yellow and a foot farther up his arm was a tattoo of the Roman Eagle. He'd picked it up in some long-forgotten place while on a drinking binge that lasted two days and did nothing at all to help him forget the horrors of the nasty little war he had just finished. So it was all the more ironic that he could never remember actually getting the tattoo, and every time he looked down at the black and blue eagle it produced a shock that it should somehow have found its way onto the arm of an officer and a gentleman by proclamation of the Emperor.

He wore his uniform as if it were part of his skin, but all his civilian clothes looked as if they were Salvation Army rejects, loud, ill-fitting, and generally inappropriate for the occasion. Across his left chest were row upon row of campaign ribbons and two or three medals for what others called heroic actions but he privately viewed as moments of absolute foolishness. He had long since learned that a soldier's life alternated between mind-numbing boredom and heart-stopping terror.

He had mixed feelings about war. As a young man he had eagerly sought dangerous situations and argued for invading any country whose real estate Rome sought to acquire, but his youthful certainty had long since given way to a profound distrust of noble slogans and naive intentions. These days he realized that politicians excuse their behavior by congratulating themselves on their intentions. But he kept these thoughts to himself and quietly tried to hold on until he got in his twenty years of service and eased into retirement.

Not that he blamed politicians and generals exclusively. He also blamed civilians whom he simply viewed as naive. Cynicism came early to him as he discovered that military men were quickly forgotten when the wars were over, and if he always looked a little fatigued it was owing to the weariness that came from fighting battles started by people who never came close enough to the death and destruction to really know war as anything more than an instrument of national policy.

Finally, when he'd had a bellyful of death and begun to feel his own deadness coldly creeping around inside him, he married. She wasn't anybody's idea of a beauty queen; in fact, she was kind of plain, with listless eyes and long stringy hair, but he loved her, and she was willing to put up with dingy military housing, PX clothes, and, every two years, hitching up the U-Haul trailer behind their five-year-old car and moving on to another assignment in another godforsaken country.

Then the baby was born and for the first time, instead of taking life, he was a partner in bringing a new life into the world. After that, things were never the same for him. They fixed up the house with a little nursery that had a bassinet lined in pink, wall-to-wall dolls, and a wooden doll house that he had built himself working evenings to construct all the miniature chairs and tables to scale. He no longer stopped by the officer's club for a couple of drinks after work; in fact, he couldn't wait to get home and spend hour after hour doting on the baby girl, who had become the center of his life. Most of his friends wanted boys to carry on their macho traditions, but the truth was he was delighted that the child was a little girl because she brought out his tender side. He also knew that Caesar could never draft her into the next nasty little war, so he was quite content and most of the time life seemed quite satisfying.

They made quite a pair, the blocky, commanding military officer, and the graceful, delicate girl child. He allowed her to crawl into his lap even when it wrinkled his immaculate uniform, and when he was sure no one was looking, he would get down on his hands and knees and play pony, while she squealed with delight, kicked his sides, and pulled his hair, which was entirely too short to make a decent mane.

Sometimes late at night he would tiptoe into the little girl's room and watch her while she slept, and during those times he couldn't help being afraid. As he watched the rise and fall of her gentle breathing he would often find himself crying, just from the ache of loving this small child so much, and also from his dreadful fear that something might happen to her. It was while sitting by her bedside that he began to pray, at first awkwardly and tentatively, but then with considerable passion and an eloquence born of his fear. Because he wasn't at all sure about this religion business, sometimes he prayed to the gods of Greece, beseeching Zeus and Athena to watch over the child, and at other times, more from a sense of duty than anything, he acknowledged Caesar as Lord and invoked the protection of his so-called divine commander in chief.

Then one day orders arrived transferring the family to Roman headquarters in Jerusalem, and once again they were moving to a new assignment. By now his rank was sufficient to forgo a U-Haul in favor of Naples Moving and Storage, the new housing was comfortable enough, a good Greek tutor was quickly found, and life continued to be happy, except for those terror-filled moments when he saw the child sleeping quietly and for no good reason became unreasonably afraid that something terrible would happen to her, which led him to find out more about the Jewish God and immerse himself in the fascinating currents of religious fervor that seemed to be the national Jewish pastime.

You probably saw him there on the great feast days, trying to look inconspicuous in his Roman uniform, hovering around the edges of the crowd, watching the celebration intently, holding a little girl's hand, and trying to keep her ice cream cone from dripping on his campaign ribbons.

Then one day his dreadful premonition became terrifying reality when the child became deathly ill. One at a time the doctors came, each one with a different diagnosis, each one with a different cure, each one with an outrageous bill, until finally in despair, the commander called his Jewish friends and asked for their help. They came right away, because the Bible tells us that this Roman military commander had donated the money to build a synagogue. Now friends, if you donate the money for a dozen pews you'll make a few religious friends, and if you donate the money for a stained-glass window you'll make a few religious friends and be visited frequently by the preacher, but if you donate the money for an entire house of worship, it is very likely that you will have many religious friends and they may even name a feast day after you.

So they came, filling first the house, then the back yard, the front yard, and finally spilling over onto the sidewalks. They were praying quite loudly, debating the finer points of theology, and consuming outrageous quantities of Manischewitz wine when someone suggested that maybe this was a job for Jesus, that popular new preacher from Galilee who had done some truly amazing things.

A great debate ensued, with some religious leaders hotly protesting any effort to involve Jesus, but finally the decision was made because maybe this time they could trap Jesus into making a mistake, or even better yet, maybe Jesus would be having a bad day and fall short of a miraculous cure.

As the messengers were sent to find Jesus and bring him to the commander's house you will notice a pivotal moment in the biblical story. As Jesus approached the commander's house, the commander sent more of his Jewish friends to say, "Lord, don't trouble yourself, for I am not worthy that you should enter my home. I didn't even count myself worthy to come to you personally. Just say a word and my daughter will be healed. For I also am a person of some authority, having under me soldiers, and I say to one 'Go' and he goes, and to another 'Come' and he comes, and to my servants 'Do' and they do."

Jesus heard these things and marveled at them, turning to the disciples and the people following him and saying, "I have not found such great faith, not even in the nation of Israel." Those who were sent returned to the house and found that the sick girl had been made well.

What a surprising situation. This hardened, commanding military officer, part of the Roman occupation forces in Jerusalem, demonstrates an unexpected tenderness, an unusual perception of Jesus, an unlikely faith that even two thousand years later reminds us of a powerful truth.

All the piety and superficial religiosity in the world are useless in the face of life's difficult moments. That's the problem with religion. If we are not careful we begin to place too much confidence in our own goodness. We begin to believe that our liturgy, our finely appointed buildings, our systems of theology, our personal commitment, our regular donations, and our good intentions can save us.

Fundamentalists have convinced themselves that believing all the right stuff will get you through, and people are willing to swallow a lot of otherwise foolish beliefs in order to hold on to something. So inerrancy becomes their god. The doctrines of the Virgin Birth, the Second Coming of Christ, and a literal view of the Creation story in Genesis become the means by which we measure faith. Fundamentalists would look at this military commander and say, "Wait a minute, does he believe all the essential elements of the faith?"

Liberals, on the other hand, would cringe at his uniform, wonder about his involvement in the Military-Industrial conspiracy, suspect that he must have voted for unchristian government, and conclude that surely a radical social activist like Jesus must have nothing to do with a man like this.

All these are ways of excluding people. When we read this story it seems to be at first glance about the commander's faith. Maybe. But the stronger note is the unlikely way God's grace is given to people "outside the pale." We like to build fences to keep people out; God builds bridges to bring people in. The church is wrong when it tries to decide who may and may not be called by Christ's name, who may and may not be included in God's gracious offer of new life in Christ. Grace is often hidden and quiet. Sometimes God uses pseudonyms. In order to see how God is at work we must broaden our vision to the whole of creation instead of limiting it to our narrow world of church walls. It isn't praying in tongues or marching in a protest demonstration that demonstrate our faith, important as these may be. It isn't how many times we came to church this month or how much we pledged to the budget that will measure the effectiveness of our faith.

The new life of wholeness and joy that the grace of God offers transcends every human effort to bottle it and label it as if it were the product of a divine snake-oil salesman. Only when we see that God tears down every idol and leaves us nothing to hold on to but grace itself are we ready for a new birth. Only when our beliefs are secondary to our trust in God and God alone as a means of our salvation and wholeness are we ready to discover what Jesus called being born again.

Jesus seems to have found this faith easier for those who have no religious pretensions, and admit that they have no prior claim upon God's power. Jesus always includes, never excludes. He even includes such folks as this hardened military commander who understands authority well enough to affirm that Christ is the ultimate authority in human life.

Grace has about it this unlikely quality. It is to be found in surprising places by unworthy people. Even unlikely people like us get into the kingdom. Not because of who we are, but because of Whose we are. Blessed be the name of God, whose grace claims us *all* as God's children.

Chapter Seven

Who and Whose

The human subconscious is a slow-moving iceberg, submerged beneath fathoms of deep, dark waters of the conscious mind. The term "Freudian slip" was coined to describe Freud's belief that there were no accidents of the mind, that all thoughts are connected in patterns and only seem random and accidental. Because so much of what we think and say flows from the headwaters of the subconscious, it can sometimes be enlightening to trace a stream of thought until the source is located and explored.

One evening recently, while I was relaxing with friends, someone asked me to define catatonia. Normally I would offer an erudite, textbook definition of catatonia: a mental disorder characterized by fixed gazes, unmoving body postures, and a failure to respond to external stimuli. It isn't often I get a chance to display my psychological vocabulary.

But for no apparent reason, rather than define catatonia, I chose to respond by playfully suggesting that Catatonia was an Eastern European country near

Bavaria that disappeared in the turmoil of World War II. Its citizens were extremely lethargic people; thus, everything in Catatonia moved at a somewhat slower pace.

Even at a time when most phonograph records were played at 78 rpm (remember them?), records in Catatonia were played at 16 rpm. The national speed limit was 12 miles an hour. Weeks were 9 days long, hours had 80 minutes, and the gestation period of pregnancy was 14 months. The monarch was referred to as Your Royal Slowness, and chess was the national sport and considered somewhat reckless and dangerous in many quarters.

Every afternoon between noon and four o'clock all activity ground to a slow stop as all the citizens of Catatonia either dozed or sat in the shade and stared vacantly into space. It was during one of these afternoon lulls that Hitler's blitzkrieg swept across the small country and, after the war, that Russia absorbed Catatonia into the Union of Soviet Socialist Republics.

Normally, I would pass off my playful response as the sort of idle humor friends often use to pass the time. But I found myself remembering the mythical characteristics I had created for Catatonia and wondering why I found it so appealing. Maybe because life in Los Angeles (or even Ogden, Utah) seems to move at a frightening pace. The temptation to live in a well-constructed, nostalgic dream world is a powerful attraction. All of us grow weary of what seems to be a growing chaos, and even a middle-aged revolutionary can occasionally lapse into a journey to Catatonia.

We are all keenly aware that we live in an age of

rapid change. Contemporary society has encountered an unprecedented change of social mores and structures, and even seemingly reliable laws of nature have given way before the inexorable march of scientific knowledge.

The theories of Euclid, Descartes, and Newton, with their static universe of solid particles, of cause and effect, of objective description, have yielded to a new way of seeing the world. Now we are told that the search for a basic element, the smallest particle of matter, is a search in vain. There is no ultimate particle—only forces of energy traveling at incredible speeds, fast enough to make them feel hard, like an airplane propeller chopping its way through air, moving so fast that air becomes hard. Science now knows that things are only fields of energy in relationship to one another. What we have thought of as substance, solid, certain, and fixed, is actually relational, fluid, relative, and flexible.

Not only has the new physics affected our scientific world view, but also moral thinking has been equally challenged by ethicists who argue against a fixed set of rules and challenge any set of givens in a situation. Instead, they challenge us to a contextual ethic that emphasizes connections between and among us. Practicing theology creatively requires a new fluidity that challenges us to listen to prophetic voices being raised that call God's people into new relationships with one another. Women, persons of other races, gays, lesbians, and oppressed peoples in developing nations are the vehicles through which God's Spirit is restlessly blowing winds of change.

The more power we have, the more we have to lose. The more we have to lose, the more entrenched we become. The more entrenched we become, the more we clutch and grasp for certainty. The more we grasp for certainty, the more idolatrous we grow. Hence, we do not live by faith and there is no room for grace in our lives. This is not to imply that every change is a good one, nor would I argue that every new idea to come down the pike must be embraced, but I do believe that the grace of God can enable us to live creatively even when uncertainty seems overwhelming. It is natural to want something to hold on to. It is understandable that we want God to be "the same yesterday, today, forever." Unfortunately God cannot be so easily corralled. Although it is true that God's essence does not change, God acts in new ways for new situations. We can believe that God is loving, merciful, just, and redemptive, always and forever. But how these divine qualities are expressed can only be determined as we see God acting in the swirl of human history.

I am a relatively young man (although my children find forty to be impossibly ancient), and even in my short lifetime incredible changes have occurred. I grew up in a society where drinking fountains, restaurants, rest rooms, schools, and residential areas were clearly delineated "Colored" and "White." Women stayed in the kitchen, children kept quiet, America would make the world safe for democracy, and God would always be on *his* throne.

All these ideas have now been challenged. In the midst of this widespread destructuring, there has been a phenomenal rise of religious fundamentalism among all faiths and in all denominations. Foreboding apocalyptic imagery is often misused to compound our fears. Even a recent United States President at one time said, "We may be the generation that sees Armageddon," a reference to biblical events commonly associated with the end of time.

Indeed, it is possible to read the Bible through lenses of fear. There are plenty of seemingly strange biblical passages about blood on the moon, signs in the sun and the stars, nations in anguish, people who faint from terror as the heavenly bodies are shaken, earthquakes, famines, and pestilences in various places, fearful events, and great signs from heaven.

In the small Southern church where I grew up, there was much talk about the world ending soon and Jesus returning to earth. This event was called the rapture. Have you ever heard of the rapture? It is the idea that the world situation will become so intolerable that Jesus will return secretly to the earth and snatch away faithful Christians. They will just disappear. I can still vividly remember, as a boy, coming home from school to discover that my mother was not at home. Of course, I told myself she had just gone to the store, or was visiting next door, but deep inside I feared that she had been taken away by the return of Jesus, and I, wicked child that I was, had been left. For several years, any time I could not find my mother, I would almost panic, believing she had been taken by the rapture. I soon devised a fail-safe method for allaying my anxieties. I would volunteer to babysit my younger brother, confident that Jesus would not leave behind an innocent baby.

Remember the runaway best seller *The Late Great Planet Earth,* which has now sold thirty million copies? Hal Lindsey dramatized the "rapture" through the words of someone who is left behind: "There I was, driving down the freeway and all of a sudden the place went crazy . . . cars going in all directions . . . and not one of them had a driver. I mean it was wild." It is also frightening.

How ironic it is then that the authors of the biblical apocalyptic passages are attempting to express to their original readers an utter confidence in God. They employ a wide variety of allusions to catastrophe and change, often using metaphors to express what would otherwise be inexpressible in human language. There is no doubt that a period of great change is anticipated. To attempt to interpret these cataclysmic events literally and date them accordingly, however, is fruitless and extremely frustrating. It also seems contrary to other scriptural injunctions that warn against predictions.

But more important, if we ask what was the purpose of these passages and how would the original readers have understood them, then we discover that beneath all the talk of change and destruction lies a deep and clear note of faith in God. "Do not be frightened" is repeated again and again. That is the clear purpose of this strange and forbidding scriptural material. Do not be frightened. Do not be anxious. Go ahead and live your lives creatively, redemptively. God can be trusted. Grace is at work.

Very little is certain, but one thing is enduring: God's love for this creation. God's grace has always been poured out upon human beings in extravagant and surprising ways. Throughout history God has been active, and we may confidently assume the future is held in the loving arms of God. This bedrock affirmation allows us to keep faith vital and creative. I no longer believe that those I love may suddenly disappear into thin air. But I believe in watching vigilantly for Christ's presence among us. Once upon a time the scriptures were used to justify all manner of human prejudice. Slavery was defended with scripture. The inherent inequality of the races was discussed in solemn, certain tones with scripture glibly quoted. Women were subjugated to men and scriptures used to chain them. The persecution of homosexuals all too often has been cultivated by frightened men and women, led by ordained homophobics. The fires of aggression and war have too often been fanned from the embers of insecurity. Sacred scriptures have been used as fuels for fears.

The clear scriptural thrust is: Do not be frightened. Do not be anxious. Go ahead and live your lives creatively, redemptively. God is at work in human history. Look expectantly for the signs of Christ among us. God can be trusted. These are the words of grace. And because we are people of grace, if we live and act in faith, even the imperfections of our momentary achievements somehow become part of God's perfection.

Each Sunday morning in our service of worship we call our children forward to the chancel steps for a sermon especially designed for them. I am reasonably confident preaching to adults, because they have been conditioned to be nice to preachers. Even if it's bad, they will probably smile and say, "I sure did enjoy that sermon." I am, however, terrified of preaching to children. They don't just tell you when it's bad. They squirm, spit, stick out their tongue at you, pinch the kid next to them, and talk back to you if you don't get the point across in clear language and reasonably quick. So of course, I allow one of my associate pastors to handle the children's moment in worship. John Rice is absolutely brilliant at this. He uses a technique that petrifies me Sunday after Sunday. Each week a different Sunday school class is given an empty bag and asked to place an object in the bag and bring it to worship. Then at the appropriate moment he is given the bag, and without knowing what is inside, he reaches in, extracts the object, and relates the object to our scripture lesson for the day. You'll never see me doing that without twenty hours of study and a script in front of me. It is uncanny to watch him work with unpredictable situations.

One Sunday morning the lectionary reading had been full of a passage from the book of Revelation that could disturb the dreams of even Catatonians. Remember them? John reached into the bag as the children watched him expectantly, and pulled out a student identification card. As usual I saw no hope for meaningful correlation, chuckled quietly, and thanked God he was on the spot instead of me.

Without missing a beat, he said, "You know kids, today we read about a lot of frightening changes that might come someday. Scares me; how about you? But what do you do when you are afraid?" He held up the ID card. "You remember who you are. Never forget that. When you're scared, when things seem to change, and they always do, remember who you are. More importantly, remember *Whose* you are. You belong to God. Nothing can change that. Nothing can separate you from God. Not ever."

That's the kind of grace we need for these changing times. Knowing who we are and Whose we are.

Chapter Eight

On the First Day

This is about grace and death.

It is sort of a parable. Be patient with it.

It was before the first day; there is no good name for it, nor had anyone even yet thought of names. It was before . . . before time was measured by sundials and watches.

There was nothing, except God of course; pure essence and being beyond being, but growing a little restless, and occasionally even perhaps slightly lonely.

It was before the first day. Before darkness and light were unevenly hewn and forged into separation except for those few moments when they seemed to kiss each other good-bye at dusk and embrace in a warming hello at dawn.

It was before snakes and frogs, turtles, flowers, freeway traffic, Fifth Avenue stylishness, and California sunburns. In fact, California wasn't thought of yet either, so there weren't any personalized license plates. There was no TV to mush your mind, for which

God was grateful, and not even any Haagen Dazs chocolate chip ice cream, for which God was infinitely sad. And realizing how much time would be required to move from Adam to ice cream, 15 billion years being a long time even for the Lord of the Universe, God got busy creating, and soon all the divine activity, huffing and puffing and whizzing all around, produced a cosmic explosion the likes of which had not been seen, and before you could say three billion years, it was the first day.

Little happened for the longest time, but finally, stirring around beneath the vast waters, undisturbed by skiers or cruise ships, something began to stir. The watery cocoon was just perfect to beat back the ultraviolet rays of the sun, but not so deep that the pressure would crush the fragile life forms that began to emerge. Out of all the chaos and crud, God created life, simple at first, but, with well-developed mothering instincts, God waited and patiently nurtured the simple life forms into complex creatures. And before you could say a billion years, there were creatures running around with a strange resemblance to folks like us, only more in need of haircuts, toothbrushes, and soap. The first day had begun, and God said this was all pretty good, but a long way from ice cream. Still, it was a good beginning.

Things went along pretty well, and even religion began to get interesting, with a swirl of contradiction and controversy. Oh, sure, creeds and beliefs got in the way sometimes. Priests were what was most annoying about the whole business God thought, with their preening and posturing, and spewing forth of nonsense most of the time, but people hung on to faith despite their crazy holy shamans, and God decided you probably couldn't get rid of priests altogether, so the next best thing was to keep them a little crazy and maladjusted. Then, in a moment of sheer divine brilliance, God suggested that maybe these holy types shouldn't marry lest they propagate the earth like a plague of locusts and strip away the tender blossoms of pure, colorful plurality. God by now was absolutely delighted with diversity and enjoyed watching it spread across the face of the earth like bright spring flowers whose erratic colors bring a smile to even the most jaded heart.

There were of course a few glitches, priests being only one of the problems God had encountered after the first day began. Death had entered the picture, bringing with it a shriveled, icy hate, as lifeless and cold as an arctic morning. God could see right through death of course, and beat the sucker at arm wrestling any day of the week, because by now there was not only the first day, but also six brothers and sisters to help define things and keep order.

Death bothered God—a lot—mostly because it was so frightening for the children of the world. Adults are naturally anxious and confused, always were, probably always will be. God knew that. But kids are close to God's heart, and the truth is, God loves even adults as if they were kids, which is called grace. So finally, sometime after the *first* first day, God got busy. That's what happens when God is perplexed about something. God gets busy, which is intended as a lesson for us all.

Using a problem-solving approach, which took a little time, in which first the problem was clearly defined, then possible solutions outlined and carefully evaluated, God, like all good authors, decided not to use a heavy hand, which would only have destroyed the plot and violated the integrity of the characters. So God became a part of the story. In a wonderful, creative approach to the problem, God decided to use something that would later be called "management by walking around."

The Gospel of John says, "The Word became flesh and dwelt among us" (1:14 RSV). It is a mystery better than anything by Agatha Christie, Raymond Chandler, or even Boston Blackie (which somewhat dates me). It is a mystery better than anything you are likely to run across again, and full to the brim with awe and surprising joy. God became flesh in some fashion that we still do not fully comprehend, but, priests and preachers being what they are, we stutter our way through sermon after sermon pointing to Jesus anyway, and saying, "Look, just look, this is what God is like." Of course, you can't see everything there is to see about God, but if you look closely at Jesus you can see enough of God walking around to believe that anytime, anywhere, at any moment, mystery may invade your life and leave you breathless and wondering and glowing with anticipation for life's next surprise.

And then, of course, after growing up as every boy and girl grows up, taking out the garbage, trying unsuccessfully to keep his room clean, failing his driver's license exam the first time, getting several C's on his report card, and suffering through Joseph and Mary's endless lectures about brushing his teeth and always wearing clean underwear to the synagogue, Jesus strode all about that tiny, unlikely country called Israel, creating more of a fuss than anyone could have expected, especially his poor mother, who had hoped the boy might turn into a good Jewish doctor. But why endure medical school, Jesus thought, when you can radiate a wholeness whose tender touch brings healing and strength to those who are sick. The poor, the dispossessed, the cast aside, the ignored, the victimized, the lonely, the misbegotten, the queer, the hungry, those whose arms and legs were rotting away, all these and more crowded in upon Jesus until the clamor and the agony at times suffocated him. Most people thought Jesus was nothing short of incredible, and some said nothing short of the Son of God. Priests weren't happy, but then again, they always suffer from terminal criticism, and even God can't please 'em.

For three short years, Jesus was among us and history has been his story ever since. We were there with him, because it is our story too. He preached like no one before or after, including Harry Emerson Fosdick. Didn't raise his voice a lot, didn't use big words; in fact, mostly seems to have told stories, some of which are hilarious, some of which are quite poignant, and all of which can cut you to the quick with insights that make them seem as if he must have been thinking of you when he told them. His days were filled with moment after moment of goodness. At night he roasted wienies around the fire with the disciples, and wrestled with them on Saturdays after synagogue, never realizing that someday Hulk Hogan would turn wrestling into a tacky little racket.

One day, after he did all that a human being can do, and did it in a short amount of time, he did what only God could do. He wrestled with the principalities and powers of darkness, pinned death to the mat, like a 97-pound weakling, and even, though it was touch and go for a while, endured the pain of the cross, outsmarted Pilate and the whole gang of politicos and priests, and came right out of the tomb with power and glory all over him and life in his eyes like the light of a new day. And it was the first day all over again. Death was conquered, life was and is triumphant.

That's why Christians get so excited about Easter. That's why Sunday is the first day, and Monday through Saturday must be content to bask in its glow. But even so there is plenty of light to go around, because Jesus the risen Savior inhabits every day there ever was or ever shall be, even the days after you and I have to face the finality of our last day.

Death still stalks around all over the place, leering and grimacing, like a vanquished wrestler, with its voice full of sound and fury. But it is a feeble squeak indeed, compared with the One who says, "I am the Resurrection and the Life."

Maybe death has the last word, I don't know.

I'll tell you what I think. I'm willing to bet my life that grace has the last word. Because it got here first.

Chapter Nine

Sin Boldly

One hot Carolina afternoon, on a visit home, my family and I were driving along when we passed an orchard of peaches that advertised especially low prices if we were only willing to pick them ourselves. I doubt that any bargain would be sufficiently attractive to me now to lure me out of my air-conditioned car and into a steamy afternoon to pick peaches, but we were younger then, poorer then, and in less of a hurry than we tend to be these days. So we pulled over, paid our money, and selected a bushel basket to fill with fresh, ripe Spartanburg peaches.

As we set off into the orchard, an old fellow, as wrinkled as a peach pit and who was tending the place, said, "If you want the best fruit, go deeper into the orchard; the peaches along the fringes are picked over, but deeper into the orchard, you'll find the best fruit." We walked a way, far enough along that I figured we had gone past the picked-over sections. But just as we set the basket down he hollered, "Go deeper." So we picked up the basket, went a little farther, set the basket down, and again we heard him shouting his advice, "Go deeper. The best fruit's farther in." Once more we picked up the basket and walked along, finally deciding that surely we were now deep enough, but once more as we prepared to pick the peaches, he hollered, *"Go on. Go deeper."* This time we went a substantially longer distance, and discovered that indeed he was right. The finest, plumpest peaches were untouched and waiting for us.

What passes for faith in our time is not much different from that experience at the orchard. So often we stay right around the edges, not trying very hard to deepen our understanding, content to lead unexamined lives where we know ourselves very little and God even less. No wonder the fruits of religious experience taste so bitter in our mouths and bring so little nourishment to the lives of people who are otherwise quite famished and searching for something that will fulfill the deepest hunger of their souls.

How is it that a message as fresh and invigorating as the one the Bible gives us becomes more like taking a dose of castor oil than biting into a juicy, refreshing peach? Perhaps it is because we pick from the rigid, moralistic trees around the outer edges of our faith and never bother to go deeper into the truly satisfying experience of a God who deals with us in love and tender mercy. At the center of the Garden, grace brings forth fruits of judgment and mercy that blossom together. What theology so often fails to hold in a creative tension, the surprising characters who inhabit the Bible illustrate in stories too good not to be true. If the mark of great literature is its ability to illuminate the complexity of the human situation, then the Bible must be ranked as a plumb line by which literature is measured.

Perhaps no other tale in the Bible illustrates this more powerfully than the story of David and Bathsheba. If it was a peach David was after, that certainly describes Bathsheba the first time he saw her. Having just finished fighting the Syrians, David was feeling restless and somewhat empty. Like all overachievers, he was better at conquering new horizons than savoring the taste of success.

In the heat of the late afternoon, David fixed himself a double scotch and walked out onto his balcony that overlooked the city. He reached down and pinched an inch of his waistline and reminded himself that he had to start using the gleaming new exercise equipment recently installed in the palace. With a bored glance, knowing he possessed all that he could see, he suddenly stopped breathing as he noticed a naked woman standing in a shallow pool dripping water over her shoulders with cupped hands. The sweltering afternoon seemed cool in comparison with the flash of heat in his loins. His passion buckled his knees, and to try to quench his suddenly dry, parched throat, David tossed down the whole drink and coughed a bit as either the scotch or the woman's beauty caught him off guard.

Like all overachievers, David was always looking for new horizons to conquer, and Bathsheba looked like just the kind of new horizon a king might want to explore. It wasn't just her naked sensuality as the water poured across her lovely olive skin that David couldn't take his eyes off of, nor was it simply that having seen so much of death he needed some warmth and tenderness to make him feel alive again. What buckled his knees and caused him to gulp the drink was the sudden overwhelming desire to have her at any cost and the fear that the cost would be quite high indeed.

What really shocks us is the fact that, not only is this a story from the Bible, but also David is the greatest king of Israel and the author of some of the most cherished religious poetry of all time. "The Lord is my shepherd" may ring a bell even for those of you who seldom enter church doors between Easter and Christmas.

If we were honest with one another, we would probably prefer that the biblical writers had chosen to leave out the story, because generally we still like our religious leaders to be above reproach. To our enlightened ears the story sounds more than a little sexist, perhaps even bordering on being an account of rape. But it isn't just David the king that concerns the Bible, nor is it David the psalmist that we see here; rather, it is someone more akin to ourselves, David the human being whose knees buckled as the lovely, naked woman innocently, sensually tried to bathe away her sweaty afternoon.

The relationship that began with adultery was consummated in the murder of an innocent man. Although the first child of David and Bathsheba died, as if no good could come of such a liaison, in time a child named Solomon was born to them, but not before the Prophet Nathan came to David with a story within a story that once again buckled David's knees and had him reaching for a stiff shot of scotch.

Nathan told a cleverly apt parable about a rich guy with thousands of sheep who killed a poor man's pet lamb and served gyro sandwiches to his friends. Then Nathan launched into a sermon that gave new meaning to the word *guilt* and inspired Jewish mothers for a thousand years. By the time he finished, David had decided to cancel all his appointments for the rest of his day and slither away to lick his wounds, which by then were numerous.

Usually, as the story has been preached and retold by thousands of years of preachers and Sunday school teachers, here ends the sordid tale. David and Bathsheba, no one's idea of Methodist Man and Woman of the Year. This story has it all: lust, adultery, even murder, as God's eternal soap opera, "All My Children," continues next week. Their baby Solomon would grow up to be renowned for his wisdom, and eventually, chip off the block that he was, would write the least-mentioned book of the Bible, a bawdy bunch of poems called the Song of Solomon.

Usually we tell the story to make our moralistic illustrations about sin, and God knows it has sin enough for any television series. And, if the story ends here there isn't much else to say, so all of us decent church-going types can shake our heads and pray that next Sunday the pastor will get back to the gospel so the worship service will be safe for children again.

Whatever sins we may have committed are all safely hidden or forgotten and thank God prophets like Nathan, with their pointed stories, are few and far between. The problem with plastic saints who tell about their triumphs over sin using the past tense and saying wisely, but with the right tone of sadness, "Yes, I was once a sinner," is that we miss the most important point. It isn't that plastic saints are somehow not sinners anymore, it is rather more likely that our sins are so much more subtle and, thus, potentially more destructive and corrosive than ever. If your knees haven't buckled recently from a sudden surge of raw desire and if you haven't done anything stupidly, flagrantly wrong in years, that doesn't necessarily mean God will award you with a plaque for the Christian most likely to succeed. It may mean nothing more profound than that your life is lived so cautiously and with such great control that even if God wanted to help you there would be no need, because you are managing quite nicely, thank you very much.

If it doesn't do anything else for us, religious faith ought to take enough of the plastic out of our lives that we become real to one another and real to ourselves. The more subtle and hidden sin becomes, the harder it is to get past it. Sins of the spirit are no less sins than those of the flesh, and maybe our reactions to the story of David and Bathsheba are more like those of the fellow Jesus pointed to who was praying in the temple. Remember? The man said proudly, "I thank God that I am not like other people."

So it is that Martin Luther could say, "Sin boldly . . . but trust God more boldly still." Just to show you that that is shocking advice, when I displayed the title of this sermon on our church's sign that fronts one of the city's most traveled boulevards, several persons took the time to check and be sure that this was the correct sermon title. One person called the church to help us out before we got too embarrassed by the sign. He told my secretary, "You left off the *g*," presuming that I had meant to call the sermon "Sing Boldly."

"Sin boldly, but trust God more boldly still," said the father of the Protestant Reformation. By which he meant that religious faith should help us see ourselves honestly, and that if we're going to play games with God, Hide and Seek won't get us anywhere. The problem with our tendencies to posture and pretend that we are better people than we really are, is that our moralistic games leave us lonely, insecure, and worst of all, unforgiven.

The question that confronts us as we pick around the edges of the orchard, is this: "Which is stronger and more enduring, sin or grace?" How strong is God's grace? How enduring is God's mercy? How deep is God's love? If the moral failures of our lives have the power to put us beyond the reach of God's gracious offer to love us and heal us, then grace isn't very strong at all.

It seems to me that Luther's wise advice to sin boldly, but trust God more boldly still reminds us that whatever holiness we may have is not of our own doing but comes to us as the gracious gift of God, and just to remind us of that, God came to us wrapped in the clothing of human flesh. When Jesus willingly gave himself to be killed, the point was made forever that God is big enough and has watched the human

107

soap opera long enough to love us with a passion that could buckle our knees if we once understand it.

Without blinking at sin, without denying it or rationalizing it, the Christian faith reminds us that sin is not the last word. The final word, the eternal word is *grace*. I think we can take sin very seriously, never blink at it, and still proclaim with joy that God must love sinners, 'cause God made so many of them (to borrow and adapt the saying of Abraham Lincoln). Deeper into the orchard of faith we find that, in fact, the moments of our greatest sin are the moments of God's greatest opportunity. Our faith is not about candles and liturgy, altars and stained glass; our faith is about living creatively, sometimes failing, often falling short, but going on with our lives anyway, and who knows what God can create out of the mess that we make of things.

Just in case you've always heard that the story of David and Bathsheba ended in the book of Samuel, and just in case you thought they were a hopeless couple of adulterers and murderers, let me finish the story as the Bible tells it, and let's see what God created out of this mess.

The book of the genealogy of Jesus Christ, the son of David, the son of Abraham.

Abraham was the father of Isaac, and Isaac the father of Jacob, and Jacob the father of Judah and his brothers, and Judah the father of Perez and Zerah by Tamar, and Perez the father of Hezron, and Hezron the father of Ram, and Ram the father of Amminadab, and Amminadab the father of Nahshon, and Nahshon the father of Salmon, and Salmon the father of Boaz by Rahab, and Boaz the father of Obed by Ruth, and Obed the father of Jesse, and Jesse the father of David the king.

And David was the father of Solomon by the wife of Uriah, and Solomon the father of Rehoboam, and Rehoboam the father of Abijah, and Abijah the father of Asa, and Asa the father of Jehoshaphat, and Jehoshaphat the father of Joram, and Joram the father of Uzziah, and Uzziah the father of Jotham, and Jotham the father of Ahaz, and Ahaz the father of Hezekiah, and Hezekiah the father of Manasseh, and Manasseh the father of Amos, and Amos the father of Josiah, and Josiah the father of Jechoniah and his brothers, at the time of the deportation to Babylon.

And after the deportation to Babylon: Jechoniah was the father of Shealtiel, and Shealtiel the father of Zerubbabel, and Zerubbabel the father of Abiud, and Abiud the father of Eliakim, and Eliakim the father of Azor, and Azor the father of Zadok, and Zadok the father of Achim, and Achim the father of Eliud, and Eliud the father of Eleazar, and Eleazar the father of Matthan, and Matthan the father of Jacob, *and Jacob the father of Joseph the husband of Mary, of whom Jesus was born, who is called Christ.*

So all the generations from Abraham to David were fourteen generations, and from David to the deportation to Babylon fourteen generations, and from the deportation to Babylon to the Christ fourteen generations.

A Concluding Unscientific Postscript
(With apologies to Kierkegaard)

Only now, at the end of this work, do I realize how deeply my own life and ministry have been inter-twined with the message I have tried to convey here. I am somewhat embarrassed that at times I seem to have lapsed into narcissistic auto-biography. But at the final analysis, I'll stand by it; my truth is really all I have to offer you. For many reasons I have struggled to accept my own acceptance, usually feeling that somehow I've had to work hard to earn my way through life, which isn't all that bad as a character trait, but has often cost me a sense of joy. Were it not for my children, my church, and a few good friends, I would never remember to celebrate life and savor its surprising gifts. The nice thing about a gift is that you can't earn it, and you seldom deserve it. Maybe the classical theologians weren't too far wrong in their definitions of grace.

I originally started a Ph.D. program in psychology because I wanted to offer my parishioners the skills of a trained counselor. After several years of study in the field, I have come to realize that technique doesn't heal, only grace heals. So often as I listen to their stories, and more painfully as I examine my own story, I am keenly aware that when any doctrine except grace is made central to the gospel a distortion occurs, wholeness is shattered, and dis-ease results. We all make dumb choices, fall on our faces daily, and sin when we think no one is looking.

Too many Christians today caricature God as the angry, vengeful Yahweh of the Old Testament instead of connecting the process by which God judges us to the grace by which God transforms us into Christlikeness. Central to all that we know about God is love. Grace is the means by which that love is fully expressed. Any good counselor knows that nobody changes until he or she is first accepted. Every action may not be acceptable, but the person must be.

I can still remember my mother reading those wonderful stories from the New Testament that remind us of Jesus' healing ministry. Everywhere he went people found hope and wholeness. He never pointed to any one person and called that person a sinner. *Never.* I dare you to find one example, and if you do, write me and I'll recant. In fact, the strongest words of Christ seem to be reserved for the religious people of his day who made faith difficult and God a distant Judge who kept very thorough records. No wonder the common people heard Jesus gladly; they still do, for that matter.

Even now, in my post-Bultmann days, when I read the stories of the New Testament I marvel at the

111

graciousness of Jesus. He would say, "Your faith has made you whole. Get up and walk." Jesus made it look so effortless that, as a child I thought, "If it's that easy why ain't everybody healed." It's something I wonder about to this day.

Perhaps at least part of the reason is that we have not been faithful to our heritage of grace. It has always been central to the understanding of theology in the Methodist tradition, but sadly not always prominent in our official pronouncements. In this era of turbulence and downright meanness, grace is more needed than ever. Increasingly, mainline churches have relinquished apologetics to television evange- lists, who too frequently preach a gospel singularly devoid of grace. Nor have we mainliners always been willing to live with the radical implications of grace for human existence. Sometimes, these days, we seem too ready to jump on bandwagon Christianity and exclude those whose sins appear to be more odious than ours. Someone said it's like walking through a hospital and shouting, "The problem with you people is that you're all sick." Maybe so. The good news is: Grace heals.

Grace to you.